# THE DILEMMA OF SECLUSION AND INNER SPACES IN THE NOVELS OF SHASHI DESHPANDE

# THE DILEMMA OF SECLUSION AND INNER SPACES IN THE NOVELS OF SHASHI DESHPANDE

Deepali Sharma

AUTHORSPRESS

Worldwide Circulation through Authorspress Global Network
**First Published in 2022**
**by**
**Authorspress**
Q-2A Hauz Khas Enclave, New Delhi-110 016 (India)
Phone: (0) 9818049852
E-mail: authorspressgroup@gmail.com
Website: www.authorspressbooks.com

**The Dilemma of Seclusion and Inner Spaces in The Novels of Shashi Deshpande**
ISBN 978-93-5529-135-6



Printed in India at Thomson Press (India) Limited

# Preface

Broadly speaking, seclusion refers to isolation and aloofness. A secluded person is away from society – residing in a detached corner. It is a universal phenomenon which implies to individual feeling or state of dissociation from self, from others and from the world at large. The most significant consequence of seclusion is the inner space. The loss of faith of the sense of belongingness lays emphasis on the existence. Being a non-entity, contemporary woman strives for her well-defined place in society and family. Several writers of the twentieth century look concerned about this dilemma of woman. The Indian English feminist novelists are no exception to it. They give vent to this feeling faithfully in their novels. Shashi Deshpande (1938-) has also executed the certainty in her novels that woman can only pretend to be contended and gratified but this pretense only leads to seclusion and loneliness. This crucial sense of detachment, absence of interaction and destitution of self-esteem act powerfully in her novels. Shashi Deshpande is a woman writer, who writes about women. Most of her writing comes out of her own intense and long suppressed feelings about what it is to be a woman in our society. It comes out of the experience of the difficulty of playing different roles. Her writing comes out of her consciousness of the conflict between her idea of herself as a human being and the idea that society has of her as woman. As a woman writer she deals with gender-related experiences. Shashi Deshpande's novels are concerned with woman's search for inner space, an investigation of psyche and an understanding of the mysteries of life and the protagonist's place in it. Indian women suffer, submit and adjust themselves to the circumstances. The novelist has projected this aspect of Indian woman with more sensitivity and instinctive understanding as she belongs to this category, in the sense that, unlike other women writers, she is born and brought up on this soil, got her education in this country itself and wrote about India. Her novels deal with the Indian middle-class woman's sufferings, dilemmas, frustrations, social agitations, and their stillness in matters of communication. Her emphasis is on woman's consciousness of herself as individual subject growing through her dependence on others, rather her seclusion from them. Woman's unconscious responsiveness to those she meets, enables her to learn personal likes and dislikes, how she communicates or hides emotions, and what motivates her to act or stay still. Some people do not feel wholeness in their self. Shashi Deshpande's novels begin with a character starting to discover this lack of wholeness because some unexpected is there to turn her life upside down. Her novels offer a startling vivid perception of the inner world of Indian womanhood, forced to remain silent for a very long duration of time. These dilemmas are sometimes subdued and sometimes elaborated. Due to non-communication, Shashi Deshpande's protagonist feels herself secluded. Lack of communication enhances this feeling. This feeling in woman characters leads to the necessity of search for inner space. The search of identity 'who am I' is an ever present phenomenon. The sense of seclusion, however, is neither destructive nor depressing. It is constructive and is an integral part of human life. It is a phenomenon that woman protagonists of Shashi Deshpande must live through. It is positive and urges woman to find meaning in life since life is real and earnest. Life is complex for the major woman characters of Shashi Deshpande. If one finds not hope from the feeling of seclusion, she needs not be in a state of morose, helplessness and dejection. Seclusion motivates woman to evolve a strategy for survival, to launch a search to find her real self. Shashi Deshpande catches on the subtle psychological complexities of the individual mind. She possesses a keen insight into complexities of human behaviour, probes oneself more than the others self, finds herself with the crisis of day-to-day life, in search of meaning and purpose of life.

**Deepali Sharma**

# Contents

# CHAPTER 1

# The Making of the Novelist Shashi Deshpande

## 1.1 Feminism

In Indian federation, the axiom is globally accustomed that woman is physically and mentally equipped to perform equally with man. She has not only been denied to colonise as a complete human-being, but also deprived of the opportunities to give expression to her ideas, instincts and anguish. The woman, an inaudible bearer, is for ages waiting for emotional release. The function conveyed to man and to woman is one of the most structured patterns of Indian society. Woman is the follower, man the leader; woman is for the home, man of the world. Not only she has been defined as a subject in her own authority but merely has an entity which deals with man either in his realistic or visionary life. Feminism is a serious attempt to formulate the issues and find solutions to gender problems. Feminist progression, started in 1960s in West went a mile long route in arresting the injustice allocated to woman. Feminism, in universal phrase denotes the advocacy of woman's right to entire citizenship that encompasses financial and social equality with man. It is a radically confronted phenomenon insofar as no general agreement exists about its boundaries. Due to gender discrimination, woman undergoes social, personal or economic biases that are also included in it. According to the encyclopedia of Lexicon: "Feminism encompasses some widely differing views however, including those which advocate female sectarianism"[1]. Feminist arguments regarding justice for woman have nothing to do with the extent to which man and woman are parallel or different by nature. The socially contrived differences in situation of male and female are the matter of concern for them. These differences put the woman in an artificially worse state. Subordination of woman in family and society with man's claims to define what is good for woman without consulting her has been opposed by feminism. Hence, it controls mechanism and challenges patriarchal thought and social organisation.

Although radical, socialist, Marxist, lesbian and sub-groups are the remnants of feminism but have an essential unity which has been derived from a potential identity among women. This identity is based on the very concept that women share equivalent experiences. The situations such as economic oppression, legal discrimination and an intrinsic reply – the feelings are approximately same to all women. Woman's organisation is seen as an expression of this community of feeling and experience. According to Gur Pyari Jandial, "there are two institutions of feminism: The object of older institute is restricted to the concept of equality in political and civil rights, occupational opportunities, positions and remunerations"[2]. The modern feminists who belong to the second institute emphasise on individual human rights and the quest for personal independence, dismissing socially defined roles. She says that "Feminism and woman's movement are inseparable. Feminism is an ideological product of certain economic and social conditions." (A Feminist Tradition, 109) In the last few years of the twentieth century, the movement for the liberation of woman emerged with a new explosion of energy and strength. Traditional attitudes towards woman have come under attack everywhere; legal battles have been fought and won and the serious and sustained attention to the matter of woman has been given by mass media too. Suddenly, the woman question has emerged as a matter of public discussions and awareness. This can be partly attributed to Simone de Beauvoir's *The Second Sex,* which first appeared in English in 1952 and had a tremendous influence on the whole generation of man and woman. It still remains as a powerful awareness-raising work.

The origin of modern feminism took place in twentieth century with the major democratic obliterations. Karen Offen, a leading feminist critic, considers that different strands of feminism can be grouped into two arguments: relational and individualist. The first one proposed a gender-based but universal vision of social organisation. It stressed on woman's rights as woman. On the other hand, individualistic arguments lay emphasis on individual, irrespective of gender bias. It emphasised more on abstract concepts of individual human rights and dismissed socially defined roles. Although these two are different but intertwined in most feminist articulation.

Till 1960s, the woman's movement did not emerge when the pattern of civil rights movements and dissatisfaction of college-nurtured woman congregated. The national attention towards woman's plight was mobilised by Betty Friedan's *The Feminine Mystique* (1963). It was the founding of the national organisation of woman that provided a focus on the struggle for the rights of woman. Although, in early 1980s, the era was defeated but the right to abortion came under attack, and growing numbers of woman was seen finding the extemporisation employment measures deficient to guarantee equality. The woman's rights compelling to financial equality were made by the decline in alimony and child support combined with increasing divorce.

After1980's feminism emerges as a thought system, an outlook to recognise world realities and also a step towards better relationships. Feminism exists as an ideology as well as a critical tool in literature. But it assumes different shades in accordance with social class and cultural variations. Jandial gives her opinion, "Feminism and its campaign against an oppressive system have left a deep impression on Indian-English writings." (A Feminist Tradition, 111) The out-stretched period from Vedic era to twentieth century saw a gradual deterioration in the status of woman from a state of respect and honour to subjugation and bondage. Although, by the middle of twentieth century the constant and slow changes in economic, social and cultural patterns altered the reality of woman's position which was further improved by the accession of social and divine reform movements. To oppose violence and denigration against woman in media, many reformers campaigned energetically. Valiant efforts were originated to curb such practices as polygamy, child marriage, purdah and sati. Reformers like Swami Dayanand did much for woman's education. On the other hand, Lala Lajpat Rai is of the opinion that woman's most relevant function is to be a mother. He recommends social reformers to have a clear clench of principles because of special adaptation of woman's body to maternity. He says that she would always be apart from man mentally as well as physically. If a girl required education it was only for her entire evolution to motherhood. But Mahatma Gandhi had totally different views. His stress on woman's participation in non-violent movement brought about an influential change. He subscribed to the notion of perfect equality between man and woman.

The impact of the western theoreticians of feminism like Simone de Beauvoir's *The Second Sex* (1952), Betty Friedan's *The Feminine Mystique* (1963), and Kate Millett's *Sexual Politics* (1970), was seen in the ultimate few decades of twentieth century. Moreover, a changed perception of woman and her state in home and society has resulted from better education, job opportunities and more consciousness of woman's rights and liberty. Germaine Greer and Sylvia Plath have also contributed to the fight against the plight of woman. The contribution of Margaret Drabble, Doris Lessing, Iris Murdoch, Marilyn French and Margaret Atwood in the movements was substantial. They have been globally applauded as renowned feminist novelists. However, there were myriad spinster contributors like Jane Austen, Emily Bronte, Stevie Smith, Charlotte Mew, Mananne Moor and Elizabeth Bishop. But the freedom to express themselves from the core of their heart was sought at the price of giving up of so called-womanliness – sex, marriage, children and the social status of a wife. Though there are different shades in feminism one can broadly say that feminism has developed along the following lines:

1. Radical Feminism sees the oppression of women as fundamental and the most basic form of oppression. All other forms of oppression stem from male dominance. The purpose of this oppression is to obtain psychological ego satisfaction, and strength and self-esteem.
2. Liberal Feminism sees all people as equal; therefore there should be equality for all.
3. Rational Feminism challenges the notion of male/female identity of masculinity/femininity as metaphysical, constructed and concocted.

In modern Indian English fiction, feminism has fermented as one of the supreme expansions. An insistent probing manifestation of the role and distinction of woman in society is an occurrence of feminism only.

## 1.2 Feminist Novelists

The emergence of the treatment of woman in Indian writing in English has not been sudden. It has generated gradually and certain of its facets are visible in the works of earlier scribblers also. The feminine issues were even raised in the novels of Raja Rao, R.K.Narayan and Mulk Raj Anand but with a difference. Quantitative contributors like Raja Rao's *The Serpent And The Rope*, emphasised upon the archetypal and mythic image of deified woman. Apart from this, scribblers like Derozio in *The Fakir Of Jungheera*, projected the exploited, pitiable and degraded woman. Rabindranath Tagore, though actually writing in Bengali, made, in works like *Binodini,* an attempt to project the protesting woman. Projection of a wide arena of woman characters in novels and short stories from conventional to rebellious is done by R.K.Narayan but rebellion ends in defeat of one type or the other.

Soon after the attainment of independence some valiant efforts were made towards highlighting the plight of woman in Indian fiction. Conscious and sustained efforts have been made by innumerable writers in order to sectionalise the dilemma of woman from numerous angles. It is pleasant to perceive that the exertion of woman has been grappling the consideration of all major Indian contributors in English. In Indo-Anglian fiction women of letters formulate a substantial role. S. Prasanna Sree says that "Plenty of Indian novels are commendable for exemplifying woman's complexities. Through novels, woman can carve her own world. But the procedure is generally irrelevant"[3]. Novels clinch up in sanctifying the stereotypical magnanimity of the Indian woman, like patience, devotion and acceptance at whatever is given to her. The earlier scribblers exhibited the traditional image of woman like Sita or Savitri, a gadget or remorse, but afterwards as time changed, the lifelike image of woman, her non-completion and seclusion began to manifest. The initiation of prodigal English education not only originated verifiable mutation in the middle class walk of life but also propagated a consciousness and the freedom in the psyche of woman. This alone led to a romantic exigency for a privilege that wasn't cushy to procure. Therefore, the woman authoress consumed the collision between custom and the leading edge; it was an assimilation of woman cladding the clashes and exertion issuing from the concoction of the traditional and the futuristic esteem.

In the nineteen thirties Indian English fiction took birth and visualised a prosperous and undeviating innovation during the fifties and afterwards. The accession of woman scribblers to the diversity and genuineness of Indo-Anglian fiction is phenomenal. It furnishes the investigating psyche and a massive deal of human frailty. The caliber of human accomplishment can also be externalised through writing the novels. Without evaluating the work done by woman contributors, no adjudicator can analyse and do justice to Indo-English fiction. In Indian federation, woman is marginalised by giving her an auxiliary position. Nevertheless, she is a doctor, a lawyer, a novelist or a scientist; woman cannot rescue herself from ordained liabilities as a wife or as a family member. Woman novelists have taken up the agenda related to her plight and tried to give vent to the inner voice of society.

Multifarious skilful women of letters have contributed to sustain the true spirit of Indian fiction in English. Indian woman, her contrariety and dilemma against the obligator of coeval India have been inscribed by feminist novelists in some way or the other. According to Amar Nath Prasad: "Indian Women novelists in English and in other vernaculars try their best to deal with, apart from many other things, the pathetic plight of forsaken women, who are fated to suffer from birth to death".[4] Santha Rama Rau, is the precedent scribbler and the majority of travelogue charters the scribbler as it allows her freedom to observe, to work through episodic, isolated events and to record immediate responses. Rau's travel books are all along a self-reflection which results from interaction. In *Home To India* (1945), she is conscious of the fact that she is not a real Indian because a kind of alienation through distance and education had taken place. Her other travel books are My *Russian Journey*_and *Gifts Of Passage*, and she has also made successful version of Forster's *A Passage To India*, (1960). Her only novel *Remember The House* (1956), is somewhat different and rings true as she writes of things well within the range of her experience. Her writing has an ease and urbanity appropriate to the theme. She explores so gently the dividing gulf between the East and the West.

The fifties testify the dimension of Kamala Markandaya's ovation that she has given her novels the touch of globalisation. According to K.R.Srinivasa Iyenger, "Kamala Markandaya neither repeats herself, nor turns her fiction into a formula"[5]. In her novels, she efficaciously illustrates the dualistic pulls that the Indian woman is liable to – among her requirement to proclaim, her prestige as human being and her duty as a daughter, wife and mother. She also emphasises how the inequality in the economic and social order influence woman more than man. Though her protagonist Rukmini in *Nectar In A Sieve,* vindicates that with in a traditional role, she can adapt herself to other roles as a human being and not by means of seclusion and self-dissection but by the hands of augmentation and conversation, a profound self-knowledge can be obtained. Another protagonist is Sarojini in *A Silence Of Desire,* who is volitional to prevail her arduousness in her own way. Kamala Markandaya addresses about the exertion of penury and frequently hustles to provincial accompaniments. She also uses the urban space and places the East and West in an unequal economic relationship in numerous novels.

An indelible impact among woman novelists has been left by Ruth Prawer Jhabvala. She has published six novels – *To Whom She Will* (1955). *The Nature Of Passion* (1956), *Esmond In India* (1958), The *Householder* (1960), *Get Ready For Battle* (1962) and *A Backward Place* (1965), and two collections of short stories, *Like Birds, Like Fishes* (1963), and *A Stronger Climate* (1968). She was born of Polish parents in Germany, got education in English but married an Indian and for about 24 years she lived in India. Mostly her focus was on upper class north India where people are sensuous, indolent and emotional. Her portrayal of woman is very limited and narrow, which only leaves the impression of their being contemptible and pathetic. She inscribes prolifically and with versatility about personal relationships, man woman relationships and domestic life. Her portrayal of women provokes Shanta Krishnaswamy to comment that "her examples of women in her fiction seem to make people unacquainted with India believe that all Indian women are contemptible, flighty or neurotic and pathetic creatures."[6]

In the sixties, prior to the feminist agitation, another noteworthy woman contributor Nayantara Sahgal initiated her writing career. The niece of Pt. Jawaharlal Nehru and daughter of Vijayalaxmi Pandit, Nayantara Sahgal has published both fiction and non-fiction. Her novels explore delicately the surface and root of woman's sufferings. She raises the issue of rape in *A Situation In New Delhi*; a premarital relationship in *Storm In Chandigarh*; adulterous desires both in *Storm In Chandigarh,* and *The Day In Shadow;* and, in novel after novel, recognises the importance of both communication and sexual delight. She makes a close and sensitive study of her elite woman characters. Her protagonist refuses to remain fettered to her subaltern roles and defy traditional norms and values in quest of emancipation. The concept of woman as subservient to man and as man's property is deep-rooted in Indian tradition as well. In "Women: Persons or Possessions," Nayantara Sahgal wrote, "When I heard someone remark: 'we never allow our daughters to go out' or 'I can't do that' my husband would not like it', it sounded a very peculiar, alien jargon. As if, I thought, women were property, not persons."[7] In her exploration of failed marital relationships, she often sees the male desire to stamp possession on women as the core of the problem.

Another prominent feminist novelist, Anita Desai, has annexed a new extension to the accomplishment of Indian women of letters in Indo-English fiction. Her forte is the exploration of advanced Indian woman. Anita Desai's *Cry, the Peacock* and *Voices In The City*, both visible in the sixties. Broadly speaking, her women protagonists are eminently prudent and perceptive but exhausted. They are on the edge of conceptual crisis in their attempt to take care of home and children and enquire about sentient completion for them. Maya commits murder in *Cry, The Peacock*; Monisha commits suicide in *Voices In The City*; Nanda Kaul's friend is raped in *Fire On The Mountain;* and Sita in *Where Shall We Go This Summer?* is dissenting to bring her unborn child into this severe world. These novels in the act of exploring inner spaces express and contradict seclusion. It is apparent from the manifestation of her novels that Anita Desai experiences the tragedy of estrangement in the sphere on every side of hers. She provides a florid and influential gesture to it in her novels. K.R. Srinivasa Iyenger observes: "her preoccupation is with the inner world of sensibility rather than the outer world of action." [(IWIE, pp.)] Anita Desai's novels are, for the major segment, the outlet of their scribbler's confidential sentiments. Although she does not chatter much about her intimate life through her lips, she furnishes much of it with the help of the characters that pixel in her novels. Anita Desai has acquired the fame as a major feminist novelist of international acclaim for having bestowed the dilemma of tender woman characters trapped between custom and the leading edge. Anita Desai has expressed her views in an interview with Yashodhara Dalmia: "I find it impossible to whip up any interest in a mass of women marching forward under the banner of feminism."[8]

The novels of contributors like Anita Desai mark the beginning of a pivotal phase of development in Indo-Anglian fiction. It is the gradual shift from the external world to the inner world of the individual. The women of letters herald a new morality – morality not confined to physical purity. It requires accommodation of individual desires for self-fulfillment. Their attempt is to bring about a change in social milieu where woman is accepted as equals, in all respects, to man in impartial sharing of rights, opportunities and also responsibilities in the procedure of evolution of human association.

While these writers have denied that their novels have any feminist slant, they exclude that almost all the novels written by them have a strong feminist intent and the woman issues lie at the heart of all their works. Some of the common features which prove this, are the presence of certain basic themes like the complexities of man-woman relationships, specially in the context of marriage, disturbed adolescence, the attempt to break traditional moulds in which women are trapped, sexual discrimination, introspection and rejection of the dependency structure. Almost all the novels inscribed by these novelists have woman as their central character. In Elaine Showalter's view, the history of women's writing in the west can be divided into three phases, "Feminism has unfurled gradually from the past to the present day. This expansion, she says took place in three phases :( a) Feminine: the phase of representation of the predominating trend of empowered customs, (b) Feminist: the phase of deprecate against ethics and values to accelerate individuality (c) Female: the phase of self-detection and a quest for identity, most Indo-Anglian woman authoresses of the younger era included in the third phase"[9].

Expositions are altering now. Feminism has brought about an insistent and searching exploration of the role and status of woman in society. Now-a-days woman refuses being silent. The varieties of protagonists depicted in the modern Indian English novel are educated intellectuals. They analyse their lives and through introspection reach self-realisation. The attempt made by woman novelists is now to develop a female selfhood, free of guilt and social stigma. Among the modern novelists, Shobha De is very frank, outward and straight forward in the delineation of incidents. She is famous for specifying the sexual mania of the materialistic world. In 1988, her first novel *Socialite Evening,* brought her into literary lime-light. The novelist gives a perceptive portrayal of the secret depths of human psyche. Her accurate characterisation and captivating style invoke skillfully drawn vivid images. Her novels compel the reader to associate himself or herself with situations and characters. Her main works are *Starry Nights* (1991), *Socialite Evening* (1988), *Sisters* (1992), *Sultry Days* (1994), *Strange Obsession, Snapshots, Shooting from the Hip* (1994), *Second Thought* (1996), *Small Betrayal, Surviving Men, Speed Post, Selective Memory* (1998). Briefly, Shobha De tries her best to expose the moral and spiritual breakdown of modern society in which a forsaken woman longs for pleasure and desire to fly freely in the sky of liberty.

Manju Kapur, the author of *Difficult Daughter*, succeeded in winning glorious Common Wealth writer's prize for the Eurasia region. She also represents the modern era. Currently, she is an English professor in Delhi University. The novel *Difficult daughters,* was itself an outcome of her conflicts with the mother and also the fact that she was a difficult daughter. The novel is set in the pre-independence era; Virmati's story has been traced in it. She is the daughter of well-to-do Arya Samaji Brahmin parents. Virmati spent her whole life in battle against tradition, against her parents and against conjugality – the inevitable conclusion of girl's life. The concept of patriarchy, which discards a woman's voice and her freedom, was boosted in primal novels. Manju Kapur exhibits to recommend that apart from education and economic liberty, the requirement is to confront that there is much more in life than just relying on marriage, parents and other such organisations.

Another noteworthy feminist novelist Arundhati Roy, is the first Indian citizen to achieve the prestigious Booker Prize for literature and a million dollar for her debut novel, *The God Of Small Things.* This novel flicked her to international fame and made a tremendous sale globally. There are about forty different languages in which this book has been translated. She has the credit of being the first entirely home grown Indian to have this esteemed prize. In her maiden novel, the focus has been kept on man-woman relations by her. Her vision is essentially tragic. Convulsions have been testified right from tender years of infancy by her novel, *The God Of Small Things.* In the novel, Ammu breaks out her wedding because of authorities and profligate procedures of her husband. Since winning the honourable Booker Prize for her first novel, Arundhati Roy, has concentrated her writing on political issues. These include the Narmada Dam project, India's Nuclear weapons and power company Enron's activities in India. Distinguishing moral aberration among man, as socially accepted protoplasm, too, is the forte of Arundhati Roy.

## 1.3 Life, Works and Influences of Shashi Deshpande

Although not being an acknowledged feminist, Shashi Deshpande (1938-), retains a momentous milestone among the contemporary feminist novelists who concern themselves with the complexities of woman and her interrogation for identity. She is one of India's foremost novelists who explore the inner world of Indian woman. She denotes her protagonists in a lifelike mould and also the vain exertions of woman in the fast changing social and economical factor in India. The biggish aspiration behind writing the novels is to highlight contrariety between tradition and the leading edge rapport to middle class Indian woman. Woman is the ganglion of her creative world. The exigency, probation and non-completion in the traditional Indian federation are the substantial sign-post in her novels. Shashi Deshpande's exploration of female subjugation in patriarchal family structures takes on a larger dimension than the inner psychological world portrayed by Anita Desai or Nayantara Sahgal's sophisticated upper middle-class environment. As Rani Dharker says "she creates, infact, a mosaic of marriage; women come and go, aunts, cousins, mothers, mother-in-law, friends, acquaintances, each providing a different slant on marriage, a dozen sub-texts to the main text of a protagonist whose marriage is collapsing."[10] Shashi Deshpande clarifies that she has chosen to have a woman as a central character not in order to project or support some feminist position because she feels that she can write about a woman with conviction and some inner knowledge. In conversation with Sue Dickman she says: "I know women better than I know men, so perhaps my books are more about women, and that's about it."[11]

*The making of a novelist,* is a procedure that specifies about the myriad sorts of influences, experiences and observations which cannot be called a sudden happening. It is her family aura, education, social values, surroundings, circumstances and furthermore her own experiences that play a very decisive role in generating her as a novelist. In front of her readers, she exhibits her perception, profundity of thought, sensibility and experience.

In 1938, the birth of an undisputed writer, Shashi Deshpande took place in a Brahmin family. Her father, Adya Rangachar is a renowned Kannada playwright and Sanskrit scholar. Adya, a cerebral man, wrote plays of ideas and is better known as Sriranga. In Dharwad, a smaller city of Karnataka, Shashi Deshpande had a free-spirited childhood. In talking with Aditi De (Breaking That Long Silence, May 7, 2002), she memorises her growing days in Dharwad: "I had a very free, unhampered childhood. My father was very liberal. He did not differentiate between his son and two daughters; In fact, marriage never entered his agenda for us until my mother reminded him that daughters had to be married"[12]. While talking about her father with Vanmala Viswanatha, an interviewer, she told that "he was dominant, never domineering"[13]. Only thing she is sore about is that he was somewhat detached from his family and never guided them. From her father, nevertheless, Shashi Deshpande must have acquired an intellectual bent of mind scholarship and affection for reading. Degrees in Economics from Elphinstone College, Bombay and Law from the Government Law College, Bangalore, are the result of it. From Mysore University she grabbed a post-graduate degree in English along with a diploma in Journalism. In 1962, when she was at the age of 24, married to a doctor, a neuropathologist Mr. Deshpande, belonging to a conservative background. As for the primary span of her marriage and motherhood she felt very incomplete or even dissatisfied. She felt about herself not only as a woman, wife, daughter but also a human being with a mind. Shashi Deshpande initiated writing in earnest only from 1970. She has, in the thirty plus years of her writing career, authored more than twenty books, nine novels, several collections of short stories, writing for children, the screenplay for the Hindi feature film 'Drishti' and has through them addressed several social issues of coeval India. Short stories were her debut writings which were printed in several magazines. Her short stories are *The Legacy* (1972), *It Was Dark* (1986), *It Was Nightingale* (1986), *The Miracle* (1986), *Intrusion And Other Stories* (2000), *The Stone Women* (2003), *Collected Short Stories Vol.1* (2003). She has contributed to the world of literature nine novels so far. Emergence of the themes and issues in her novels was from the plight of woman at the crucifix ways of a provisional coalition, changing from traditional to the leading edge.

*The Dark Holds No Terrors* (1980), is Shashi Deshpande's first published novel. The story of the novel is revolving round Sarita (Saru), who is a cautious, self-assertive, eager and ambitious woman. She is a doctor and her life is intricately connected to her past. She has been brought up in a severely and tradition bound family. Her mother is strident and father is silent, who remains peripheral. Being indulged in her own perplexes, she grows up. Her revolutionary exaggeration against her mother presumes to be attention probing devices. Her mother is the focal point in her likes and dislikes. Saru is jealous of her brother Dhruv's disposition with in the family as the youngest and that too being a male child. Her envy ferments into guilt when the unexpected death of Dhruv took place. A guilt that she fetches on her shoulders throughout her life. Her decision to marry Manohar (Manu) proves to be an ascent hurting her mother. The dilemma as a daughter, wife, and mother and above all as a human being is visaged by her in the entire life. Saru's tormenting experience is retrospect through this novel. Saru, the protagonist suffers as a major economic and social victim of bafflement of her husband that takes the substance of sexual cruelty which has been radiantly delineated in the novel. Sadism bulged in her husband because of the sense of minority or inferiority complex and humiliation as a result of society's reaction towards higher status of Saru. This sort of antipathy is inevitable to get oscillated back in their two children Renu and Abhi. Saru returns back to her father's home in order to get away from this torture. While humping the massive burden of guilt, her brother's death, she lost her mother who died without pacification with Saru and her husband. Secluded, fragmented, segregated, lonely and alienated Saru with the support of her father, acknowledges the fact, and admits that she had not been responsible for the death of her own brother. From there the seeds of her new life begin to sprout. Feeling of actual identity that had been lost in numerous fragmented selves originates in her. Premila Paul observes, "Shashi Deshpande does not glorify women's sufferings. Though she enlists a sufficient amount of sympathy for her protagonist, it is not on the grounds of her being a female sufferer. Throughout objectivity and avoids generalisations and partial views."[14]

*If I Die Today* (1982), Shashi Deshpande's second novel, is somewhat different from the previous one. In this novel, an explicit indication is formalised by the novelist that man is the victim of his own obnoxious nature. In her novels, she migrates from down to doom. The perpetual actuality that if one dies today others die tomorrow, is instantly delineated to the readers by the novel. The novel is set in the resident quarters of a huge charity hospital where, again, there is a complete sequence of murdering, initiating with the killing of an optinium personality career. The narrator of the novel Manju set apart herself from the average woman of India that views marriage and motherhood as the supreme happiness in life. Manju resents the fact that her children play the role of a barrier to her liberty. In the novel, there are two versions of characters-people with understanding and people without understanding, of living according to the individual self. The two characters, Guru and Meera, who seem to have intellectualised their identity, live up to themselves with an objective approach to and attitude towards an anxiety-free motivating people.

A clear specification of the fact that the main cause of all human complexities is evil is shown in Shashi Deshpande's third novel *Come Up And Be Dead* (1983). A girl's school is the scenario of the novel where a string of murders takes place; teachers and students are the victim of this. Kshama Rao, school's headmistress is the chief character of the novel. By her proportion, Devyani, her cousin, is the only other full-fledged character. She is exhibited to be slightly pacified in as much as her being a housekeeper, but now, she muses about the inefficacy of identity. Others like Pratap Rao, the brother of Kshama, is mentally disturbed; her colleague like Mrs. Jyoti Raman; her student like Sonali; her mentor Mr. Mathews; the police inspector Prasad; and, the doctor Girish. Another character of this novel is Verma who is the member of Board of Governors of school. For the cause of desolation from his wife subsequently after marriage, he constructs girls of the school to serve as call girls. His tactics towards woman are quite inexpedient. In this novel, six attempts are made to murder, out of which three made on Mridula, Pratap Rao and Jyoti Raman's life are successful while attempts on Sonali, Sharmila and Devyani are unsuccessful. Sanjay either as a doer or as a concomitant participates in all of them. For instance, in Mridula's case, who has to commit suicide for being pregnant without nuptial bond and that too at the age of sixteen only. For her pregnancy Sanjay is responsible. Sanjay is also the killer of both Pratap and Jyoti. His suspicion is on Jyoti that she is familiar with something regarding his indulgence in trade of call girls, makes him kill her. Sanjay makes an unsuccessful effort to kill Sharmila who hinders him from killing Sonali. On the other hand, there is Dr. Girish. The benevolent attitude of Girish, Pratap's doctor, makes it quite tedious for one to trace his frailty. Girish acts as a collaborator in Pratap's murder. He cannot afford to let Devyani departure from him with all revelation which makes him redeem to get Devyani killed for this cause only. He makes effort to contact some murderer, definitely, it was Sanjay because Sanjay kills or tries to kill those persons who suspected about the racket in girls being carried on under the big chief Verma. In short, *Come Up And Be Dead,* projects the idea that people kill others in the state of fear.

*Roots And Shadows* (1983), Shashi Deshpande's next novel, was awarded the Thirumathi Rangammal prize for the best Indian novel of 1982-83. It is actually her first novel but was published later. It is the story of a joint family. The parallel is drawn between Akka's marriage and widowhood and Indu's married life. Indu loves her husband, Jayant but does not want to get trapped by wifehood, which may imply complete obedience, pretence and illusion. In the midst of these two women, are the lives of a childless widow Atya who is in the quest of refuge and young Mini, who is not too pretty or auspicious as to attract a match for her. Mini's father is unable to meet dowry demands. She prefers to marry much older and ugly man rather than an eccentric and unreliable Naren. All the four women put dissimilar ideas on conjugality. According to Ujwala Patil, "In her quest for personhood and fulfillment, Indu had sought escape from family relationships, but had discovered how relationships are the roots of one's being and follow one like so many shadows that make life no more substantial than a shadow – a life without identity."[15] The novel delineates the anguish and suffocation experienced by the protagonist Indu. She despite of her family wishes marries a man, Jayant of her own choice. Her father, Govind and his elder brother, Kaka were the only two persons to attend the wedding. This dissident daughter had been obliterated by Akka. Unfortunately, born out of intercast marriage, she happens to face the loss of her mother. She was barely fifteen days old when was escorted to the ancestral home. Her father was a wandering journalist. She, in her home led a life of seclusion. Indu, like Saru went into a process of disillusionment. Even her husband, Jayant was no more far from educated and controversial Indian men. This makes her recognise the truth that her real self has been sacrificed by her in the procedure to make Jayant happy. She comes back to her home in quest of inner space for herself. At home Indu is able to analyse her relationship with Jayant dispassionately. In this dilemma she feels deeply secluded from the world at large. In quest of identity, she manifests extra-marital affair with Naren, her childhood friend, to realise ultimately that it is possible to practice autonomy within the dimensions of marriage. In the end, Indu turns an authoritative obstinate, liberated and to base her nuptial bond on a different pattern.

The very first novel of Shashi Deshpande to be printed outside India is *That Long Silence* (1988). In 1991, it achieved the meritorious Sahitya Academy Award and is applauded as a masterpiece of feminist writing in Indo-Anglian fiction. It accents Shashi Deshpande's mystique amongst the contemporary writers. Sarabjit Sandhu observes that "In *That Long Silence*, Shashi Deshpande has portrayed the irony of a woman writer who is also a young house wife. Being a writer she is supposed to present her views and ideas before the society but still she remains silent probing into her past, struggling with her present and trying to establish a rapport with her future. She is an intellectual who finds herself out of place in the society meant only for men."[16] The journey of the protagonist, Jaya towards a well-defined selfhood is mired in the formidable convulsions of societal interventions. Woman conditioning to fashion oneself as per accepted norms of behaviour, suppressive and egocentric male chauvinism and continued dilemma of annexing a purpose of her life, culminate in a long silence. Jaya, the mother of two teenage children and wife of Mohan, is the narrator of the novel. Mohan, whose corrupt business practices are under inquisition, along with Jaya decided to leave their comfortable home. The children are sent on a holiday with some family friends and Mohan and Jaya went into an old flat in Dadar which belongs to Jaya's uncle. It was then that the entire procedure of self-examination commenced for Jaya. Jaya now recognises that the satisfied, rejoicing housewife that the world saw was not her real self. Mohan's profundity of thought is that fury constituted woman unwomanly. He did not want her to inscribe what she desired. On the other hand, there is Kamat, a widower and an old friend of Jaya, who appreciated her writing and understood her inner feelings. Her association with Kamat makes her comprehend that fairness has not been done to her talents. Her seventeen year old marriage, its frustrations, regrets and her intimate omissions, all these things are recurred in her mind. She got disturbed by all her fury, her muteness, submissiveness and her capabilities. As a result of this, she killed Suhasini after having gone through a period of vibrant rumination. She remoulded her creative simulation as a writer and emerged as a new-being. *That Long Silence,* highlights the grossly unequal status of women in our society. For instance Tapan Basu says that this novel is the story of Jaya, "who has spent a lifetime in surrender of her will to social mores and customs that had relegated women to a second class status."[17]

*The Binding Vine* (1992), is Shashi Deshpande's omnipotent statement concerning physical violence against woman. The novel touches on the delicate issue of marital rape and a woman's incapability after wedding to a man she does not love. It is a prodigiously prevailing depiction of woman's struggle to survive in terrible, brutal world where there is no accessible way out. In this novel, three stories are braided imperceptibly and the writer fetches up three lives which are in various manners dissimilar: Urmila, the narrator, a college teacher grieving over the death of her baby daughter, gradually reveals the stories of the other two. Through the Kannada poems, Urmila segments the mysterious life of her mother-in-law, Mira, who died at childbirth more than thirty years before the story, began. These poems bring alive to her the woman who wrote them in the seclusion of an infelicitous marriage. While eliciting the poems and diaries of Mira, Urmi comes in contact with a victim of rape, Kalpana. Kalpana is hanging in the midst of life and death in a hospital ward. Urmi, while in the desolation of her child loss reads Mira's poems. She feels pain with Shakutai (the mother of Kalpana) and it proves very helpful for her to examine her own relationship with Kishore, her husband. Kishore works for the Merchant navy; hence for the most of the time, they invest their lives peripheral with each other. Urmi fails to fill up this intervening elongation amongst them which is both physical and intellectual. The novel can be summed up in the words of Subhash K. Jha who writes in a review: '*The Binding Vine*, is one of the few contemporary Indian novels to discuss its heroine's sexuality, her passion, with a measure of unrepentant concern. In this novel Shashi Deshpande travels much further down the road in exploring the working women's needs of the head, heart and further down the anatomy, than her earlier novels."[18]

*A Matter Of Time* (1996), is one of the supreme creations of Shashi Deshpande. In this novel, she has clearly explored the life of a woman Sumi. The reflection and refraction in the elementary women illustrated by the daughters of an emotionally secluded woman is shown in this novel. This novel spans the lives of four generations of women: Manorama, Kalyani, Sumi and Aru. Catastrophe of this novel anticipates around the disappearance of Gopal from his family, who is also a chief character. He walks out on his wife Sumi and three daughters namely Aru, Charu, and Seema. This is set apart from the backdrop of miserable story of Kalyani and Shripati in the great house. Sumi returns to this house along with her daughters, when they are left alone by Gopal, their father. An unusual sort of anxiety generates between myriad characters because of Gopal's deprivation. They all try to investigate Gopal's reason. Then there is a conjugal relationship between Kalyani and Shripati. The cause for collide on the broader matters of communication in turn predominates the sequential generations. Repetition of history occurs in Sumi's life too but both Kalyani and Sumi are silent on both events. Aru is the one who is most affected by these episodes. The tragedy of her grandmother and mother make her feel thwarted. This novel is universally about Aru's quest for identity. Initially she tried to actualise Gopal to pay for what he did to her mother. She got associated with a woman activist Surekha, a lawyer by profession, to retrieve her father. Gradually, she recognises that it should make her father to go as her mother has been all alone. The end of the novel is not a remark of hopelessness but of expectations; death of Sumi is not the termination of the novel but a new beginning of Aru's life.

Shashi Deshpande in *Small Remedies* (2000), manifests her favourite theme of a woman who has disposed a delegation of self-examination. This delegation will assemble the past and the present which will cure the wounds even if it does not yield all answers. There are three prevalent characters at the core of the story. Madhu, the narrator of the novel, is struggling to stick out of the accidental death of her beloved son. He died in a bomb blast in Bombay, persuading the abolition of Babri Masjid. Madhu's aunt, Leelabai, is another empowered character of the story. She spends a very long period to work with the factory workers of Bombay by whom fifteen year old and orphaned Madhu was brought up. Leelabai's life is satisfied in exertion for marriage with a Christian Joe. She led a life of feudal activism so as to accommodate recoils in jail, and her niece, Madhu, who has been committal to inscribe a biography of Savitribai Indorekar, is an elderly classical vocalist who belongs to the Gwalior family. She is a teacher who outbursts with all caste and communal laws. The alienation of her own daughter along with the redundancy of her family comes because she wanted to live with her Muslim lover and concomitant with a destination to search an efficacious walk of life in her elected field. Shashi Deshpande, while writing of people like Savitribai and Leela, people who dared to be different, has also created characters like Munni who desperately seek the approval of society. Malati Mathur, a reviewer writes: "At the other end of the spectrum is Munni, Savitribai's daughter who turns her back on her mother and all that she stands for, in a desperate desire to conform, having encountered early in life the poisoned barbs that society levels against those who dare to be different."[19] To alloy the tragedy of mislaying her son, Madhu also conceived a gap between her relationships with her husband Som. They disjointedly quarrel with their sorrow. Each blows up with an encumbrance of guilt because it was their turmoil that took away their beloved son in to the lap of danger and death. Finally, she, by the help of her friends, got herself converged in the job of writing biography of her old neighbour Savitribai Indorekar, a singing legend. That transit her afar from Som to a small town and she contemplated it as best decoction as it would bestow with her much prerequisite space among them. So, the novelist in Small Remedies, illustrated the nostalgia, adversity and seclusion that Madhu suffers before pacifying her misery and again she perpetuates an emplacement in society, as a human being.

Shashi Deshpande's recent novel *Moving On* (2005), is the story of families. It is about the confidential lives of man and woman their love, hate, conspiracy, and controversy. A widow woman, Manjari (Jiji) who moves in to foster for her ailing father, narrates the story. She enquires the past through diary's pages extricating old memories, recasting, and feedbacks. Her present puts before her its own requirements of a rebel daughter, conning property defrauders and her lover who threatens to throw her life out of gear again. An unpredicted earnestness, twisting and turning by the means of sophisticated emotional panorama is raced by the sequential scuffle to propitiate remorse with fact and the conflagration of body with an air for fellowship. After prospecting Baba's writing and Jiji's inspections, it exhibits that the house is formulated by the pretty but reserved Mai, the mother of Jiji, who manipulates her love mercilessly. By the means of this novel, Shashi Deshpande has divulged a passionate love affair that tears away the family adrift. Manjari as a solitary woman struggles for the completion of exigency and demands of her body.

After analysing the novels of Shashi Deshpande, no question of doubt sprouts on her general reciprocation for woman. All her protagonists have acute perceptivity of their respective smothered and feltered entity in a society which is orthodox and male-dominating. Protagonists imprisoned under traditions and modernity quest for authenticity as a wife, as a mother and as a daughter. The novels of Shashi Deshpande contain much that is feminist. But her feminism is slightly different from others. Her lifelike portrayal of woman and her identity search do not leave any doubts in readers as to where her actual sympathies lie. Her novels largely cuddle of a woman's quest for self. In order to have a full-grown information concerning novelist, it is required for the readers to have an acquaintance with all the substantial transactions of her life and predominance that played a pivotal role in moulding her into a novelist. According to R.S. Pathak, "Shashi Deshpande had never identified herself with any group of writers, whether of India or abroad but she is a widely read person"[20]. Her love for Somerset Maugham was just a passing phase. The lasting impression of Jane Austen and Bernard Shaw's work upon her has been acknowledged by her. She took interest in reading Dickens and Tolstoy. Some influence of Bronte sisters, Margaret Drabble, Doris Lessing and Erica Jong was revealed by a careful perusal of her fiction. At the same time, Simone de Beauvoir and Germaine Greer stimulate her writings to which she endorses. They assisted her to put forward all her conflicts in order. Her approach towards the leading-edge contributors of India is open minded. She appreciates some excellent books like Anita Desai's *Clear Light of Day*, and Attia Hosain's *Sunlight On A Broken Column.* She does not feel a kinship with Indo-English scribblers of the leading edge. However, she calls Salman Rushdie a path breaker. In her opinion, his *Midnight's Children*, is brilliant, original and incomprehensible – A novel that altered each and every thing for Indian contributors in English. She is equally uncomfortable about being categorised under woman writer and denies being a feminist writer with a mission. Jasbir Jain specifies that as a writer, "Shashi Deshpande negotiates the margin amongst the private and public spaces and works with the actualities of life-birth, growth, survival and death"[21]. She also crosses over from the confines of gender. Her novels highlight a need to move towards self-realisation and freedom and establish new relationships with the self as well as with others. But at no stage, responsibility of being an individual has been abdicated by any character. Hence, the need to recognise the importance of gender, the hollowness of man-woman relationship, the power of culture and the value of the self. Gradually and with great diligence, as she records social history, Shashi Deshpande subverts stereotype structures to create some space for the identity of woman.

## Notes and References

1. Elizabeth Fox-Genovese. *Lexicon Universal Encyclopedia,* (New York: Lexicon Publications, INC. 1987, 1985,1984,1983).
2. Gur Pyari Jandial. "Evolving A Feminist Tradition: The Novels of Shashi Deshpande And Manju Kapur", *The Atlantic Literary Review,* Vol.4, No.3, July – September 2003, 108, here after cited in the chapter.

3. S. Prasanna Sree. *Woman In the Novels Of Shashi Deshpande: A Study.* (New Delhi: Sarup & Sons, 2003), 77.
4. Amar Nath Prasad. "A Brief History of Indian Women Novelists In English", *Indian Women Novelists In English,* (New Delhi: Atlantic Publishers and Distributors, 2001), 2.
5. K.R. Srinivasa Iyenger. *Indian Writing in English*, (New Delhi: Sterling Publishers Private Limited, 2004), 450, hereafter cited in the chapter.
6. Shanta Krishnaswamy. "Raja Rao: The Doomed Pattern of Saved Males and Doomed Females," *Glimpses of Women in India*, (New Delhi: Ashish, 1983), 356.
7. Nayantara Sahgal. "Women: Persons or Possessions," *Hindustan Times,* 19 July 1970: iv.
8. "Interview with Anita Desai," by Yashodhara Dalmia, *The Times of India*, 29 April 1979.
9. Elaine Showalter. *A Literature of Their Own: British Women Novelists From Bronte To Lessing*, (Princeton, NK: Princeton University Press 1977).
10. Rani Dharker. "Marriage as Purdah: Fictional Rendering of a Social Reality" *Margins of Erasure: Purdah in the subcontinental Novel in English*, ed. Jasbir Singh and Amina Amin, (New Delhi: Sterling Publishers Private Limited, 1995), 57.
11. "In Conversation Sue Dickman with Indian Women Writers," *The Book Review*, Vol.19, No.4, April. 1995, 32.
12. Shashi Deshpande in talking with Aditi De in an Interview. "Breaking That Long Silence", May 7'2002.
13. Shashi Deshpande in an Interview with Vanmala Viswanatha. "A Woman's World...... All The Way"! *Literature Alive*, 1/3 December 1987.
14. Premila Paul. "The Dark Holds No Terrors; A Woman's Search for Refuge", *Indian Women Novelists*, Set I, Vol.V, ed. by R.K. Dhawan, (New Delhi: Prestige, 1991), 67.
15. Ujwala Patil. "The Theme of Marriage and Selfhood *In Roots And Shadows", Indian Women Novelists* Set I. Vol: V. ed. by. R.K. Dhawan, (New Delhi: Prestige Books, 1991), 130.
16. Sarabjit Sandhu. "The Image of Woman in That Long Silence", *Indian Women Novelists* Set I. Vol: V. ed. by. R.K. Dhawan, (New Delhi: Prestige Books, 1991), 138-146.
17. Tapan Basu. "Joining A Select Club," *Review of That Long Silence*, Sunday, No.8-14, May 1988, 98.
18. Subhash K. Jha. "Coming To Terms with Tragedy," Rev. of *The Binding Vine, The Economic Times,* No.30, 1994.
19. Malati Mathur. "Rebels In the Household," *India Today*, April 3, 2000.
20. R.S. Pathak. *The Fiction of Shashi Deshpande*, (New Delhi: Creative Books, 1998), 13.
21. Jasbir Jain. *Gendered Realities, Human Spaces: The Writing of Shashi Deshpande,* (Jaipur: Rawat Publications, 2003).

## CHAPTER 2

# Filial Ingratitude

A relationship implies interaction between two persons involving interchanges over an extended period of time. These interchanges have some degree of mutuality, in the sense that the behaviour of each takes some account of the behaviour of the other. As our society is full of paradoxes and contradictions, a female is considered as a peripheral member of family, both in her parent's house and of the husband. Throughout her lifetime, she is unable to establish her roots which results in insecurity. Broadly speaking, the daughter is closest to the mother and this insecurity is rubbed on her also. According to Rashmi Sahi, "Shashi Deshpande has delved into the problem of every woman in this society where she is given a second-grade position but is expected to be the lynch pin to the family."[1] The novelist has portrayed the inner turmoil of a woman, between her knowledgeable self and the external thrust, especially of mother. It is not that the novelist has deliberately made woman the focus in all her novels. She wanted to portray the whole society, but somehow, as the characters took shape, the women characters turned out to be the protagonists. Shashi Deshpande believes that a writer gives to society a mirror image of itself, and that she presents through her novels. She shows that a child, who is not loved and cared by her parents (especially mother), is likely to develop deep rooted sense of fear, insecurity and rejection. Consequently, children are at times highly reactionary or silent. The parent-child relationship always occupies an important place in the novels of Shashi Deshpande. Usha Bande says: "In her novels mother and mother figures are not matriarchs to be glorified but the suffocative and authoritative figures to be disdained."[2] Hence, the insecurity of impressionable years manifests itself into the wrong choice of partners and sometimes landing her into unwanted situations. Saru in *The Dark Holds No Terrors,* deliberately indulges all her life into those acts which enrage her mother. In the process of moving against the flow, Saru drains herself emotionally and physically; Indu in *Roots and Shadows*, rejects Akka, the mother surrogate; and, Jaya in *That Long Silence,* wages a relentless 'guerilla warfare' (TLS, pp.169) against Ai (mother). The above central figures of the novels are educated middle class women, career conscious proud of their independent views, rebellious, non-conformist. The traditional mother appears stereotyped, oppressed, and weak.

## 2.1 Gender Differentiation

Sarita, a child with seclusion deep rooted in her soul develops a feeling of being hated and neglected by her mother. The mother is a dominating lady who tries to control others without being aware of their views and feelings. Saru is an unwanted child. Her parents have a preference for their male child rather than the female child. There is always a 'Puja' (DHNT, pp.168) on Dhruv's (Saru's brother) birthday but nothing to celebrate hers and after Dhruv's death her birthday passes over in silence. After the death of Dhruv there were no more celebrations in the house.

As a child, Saru could not understand her mother's behaviour. Mother's hatred for her and preference to brother is evident from her actions. As Shubha Tiwari observes: "Saru's character can be truly understood only in the light of psychological precepts. First, she carries with in her the sad effects of gender discrimination. Social psychology deals with the stereotypes about the two genders. Saru's feminism springs out as a reaction to this discriminatory psychological set up of society at large and her parents in particular. Secondly Saru also has the deep-rooted mentality of an unwanted child. Psychologists have dealt in detail with the mental make-up of an unwanted child. Thirdly and most tragically Saru suffers the bruises of a terrible physical trauma on her psyche."[3] The relationship between them subverts all conventional expectations one has from these relationships. Saru grows up without the traditional support structures and has no maternal role model to follow. The emotional separation between mother and daughter is not based only on their growing up and being away from narcissistic relation to reality, but also on pain, rejection, and seclusion. It is no wonder that Saru's mother is reluctant to live after her son's death. Her constant pining for her dead son and rejection of daughter causes deep and indelible scars in Saru's mind. The mother takes no particular interest in daughter's education and personal advancement. She snubs her at every given opportunity. This sense of rejection by mother fills the mind of the adolescent Saru with a feeling of hatred. The feeling is so intense that Saru retaliates and practices provoking her mother. Hence, causing a rift between the mother and the daughter. The rejection of the mother is pronounced in the novel, "If you're a woman, I don't want to be one."[4] The hostility of the mother during these impressionable years leads Saru to psychological insecurity which finds release in two ways. One is through constant and recurrent dreams and the other is through the act of defiance. The acts of defiance mostly spring from her resentment against mother and also against her husband. Recollecting her attitude, she is developing a feeling of hatred and relations towards her mother begin to get estranged. The consequence is ironical because all this increases her suffering.

The roots of gender differentiation in our society are unfathomable and Saru's mother is no exception to it: "When a mother differentiates between her own children, the boy and the girl for whom she has equally suffered and taken equal pains, there is no torch bearer then for the girl child" (Rashmi Sahi, pp.132). Saru remembers how she was treated second to Dhruv: "He is different. He is a boy" (DHNT, pp.44). Such words clarify the image of traditional Indian mother against whom Saru has to rebel all her life. S. Anandalakshmi observes: "The birth of a son gives a woman status and she invests herself in her son's fixture, creating a deep symbiotic bond."[5] Saru realises that she is a girl, uncalled for and she should have survived her brother. This kind of rejection grows day-by-day in her. Consequently, she cannot mix-up with people in any event. She feels solitariness and deeply cloistered. Suman Bala gives her opinion that "being unwanted, she loses the basic satisfaction every human being needs, a sense of belongingness."[6] An unwanted child is a perplexed child and so is Saru. She is always neglected and ignored in favour of her brother. She is neither given any importance; nor is any parental love showered upon her. Growing in this environment of hatred, hostility, and rejection, Saru nurtures the seed of rebellion with in herself. She grows up and acquires education against the wishes of her mother. She joins medical college despite her mother being drastically against the idea. Though unsuccessful, the mother tried her best to persuade her husband not to send Saru to medical college. Her emphasis is more on getting her married so that the responsibility will be over. This reflects that girls are seen as belonging to a different family and their socialisation stresses their future roles as wives. Saru's mother continuously accused her of Dhruv's death and cursed her. When the mother accuses Saru of murdering her brother, she does not deny or refute the charge, because as Premila Paul observes, "When her mother accuses her of murder, she speaks out Saru's intentions and not the deed. Dhruv's demise had always been her subconscious desire and there is a very thin demarcation between her wish and its fulfillment."[7] The childhood experience of watching her brother sink into water and die gives her a sense of guilt that she is responsible for the death of her brother. It is enhanced by her mother's words, "You killed him. Why didn't you die? Why are you alive and when he's dead?" (DHNT, pp.173). The mother had always appeared an authority figure and posed a threat to her individuality and self-will. According to R.S. Pathak, "the power that the mother exudes repels her."[8] Saru's marriage is a means to get away from mother and home. She runs away to get married to a person of her own choice. As she always feels insecure in her parent's home, her marriage to Manu is a means of that love and security which she had always lacked in life. The mother, being an old, traditional, orthodox woman, does not want her daughter to get married to a person who is from a lower caste. Saru is not ready to listen anything. Whatever the mother says, her reaction is opposite to that. This creates a huge space between them and Saru leaves the house. The intensity of hatred is so overpowering, that her mother disowns her and dies unforgiving. Saru is left struggling with her life although there is no link with her mother even when she blames her, "I hate her, sapping me of happiness, of everything. She's always done it to…… taken happiness away from me" (DHNT, pp.109).

Filial relations remain strained and the repetition 'I hate her' is a constant reminder to the readers of her bitterness. She indicates her mother of having sapped her of all the happiness, in life as well as after death. No mother can dislike her own daughter with such fervors. But Saru's mother was an exception to it. Imagine saying……. "I will pray for her unhappiness. Let her know more sorrow that she has given me" (DHNT, pp.197). Saru is surprised to know that her mother died peacefully despite having caused her so much pain. Anyone can easily be aware of the hatred between mother and daughter.

Another protagonist Indu, in *Roots and Shadows*, suffers from seclusion and loneliness because of her surrogate mother Akka. Indu is the motherless child, brought up in a huge joint family of uncles and aunts. Although she has a father, he remains on the periphery. The family is ruled by Akka, a widow who had handled everything in the family with an iron rod. She is the traditional mother figure toeing the line set by old customs, rituals, and traditions; she is the symbol of authority. Everything that happens in the house is to be approved by her. Akka is also very particular about how a girl should talk, dress, or behave. She rebukes Indu severely for daring to talk to a boy in the lone corner of a library. Indu, who had lost her mother at birth identifies throughout the novel, Akka as a mother figure. Indu is also a rebel, who takes the bold step of marrying a man of her own choice against the wishes of her family. However, like Saru, she undergoes a process of disillusionment. She had thought that marriage would give her happiness and an identity of her own, but this does not happen. When Indu revolts against Akka, her world, and her values and marries Jayant against the wishes of her, the mother bursts out at her marriage, "Such marriages never work. Different castes, different Languages……it is all right for a while. They realise."[9] Akka wonders whether such a marriage will not be an incongruous idea. In this family all things, big and small, do not go unless Akka's value is attached to them. Although Akka is a woman, all her views strictly conform to the masculine laws. Indu's hatred of Akka is not personal but is directed at her authoritarian ideas, worn-out conventional views, and superstitions and so on, shared by all simply because they were liked by Akka. In Indu's ancestral home the partition between male and female worlds is always very sharp. Woman is not allowed to join important family discussions, not even Akka. When Indu comes back to her parental home after Akka's death, she becomes the sole inheritor of her property. But Indu in the beginning refuses to accept her as a role-model and rejects Akka's orthodoxy and rituals. She carves a life of her own, hoping that by escaping from Akka she will gain independence and freedom to live as she pleases without the bounds of the family and the society. Indu is just a woman for the male family members of the house, who consider her a married woman, an outsider. To them, she has no right to inherit either money or property because she is a married woman. She is a woman that is why she is always marked. Among uneducated women folk she is a childless woman, although she and her husband opt out of getting children for personal and domestic reasons. To them, it is immaterial how educated she is and how successful she is in her profession. Every man and every woman have his or her own mode of judgement, riddled with ignorance, superstition and genderised views. In the novel, the dominant culture and the marginalised culture are displayed in the form of suppression of the latter by the former. In fact, this enters the psychology of unconsciousness that subjects woman to silence so as she does not identify herself with the masculine imagery. Indu says that "as a child, they told me I must be obedient and unquestioning. As a girl, they told me I must be meek and submissive. Why? I had asked. Because you are a female. You must accept everything, even defeat, with grace because you are a girl, they said. It is the only way, they said, for a female to live and survive……" (RS, pp.158-159)

On the other hand, there is rich, childless, psychological harassed in her youth by a much older husband, and widowed at a very young age, Akka with Sunanda-Atya, represents the two mother surrogates in the novel. Indu is much in the same mould of Akka that she becomes the inheritor of Akka's property and establishes her identity as Akka's child. Indu longs to be wanted, loved, described, and admired. She also, in an act of rebellion proposes to Jayant, although usually it is the other way round for a female. She marries Jayant; much against what Akka had ordered and leaves home: "Full of hatred for the family, for Akka specially." (RS, pp.12-18). Shashi Deshpande's heroines emerge from a conservative, middle class, society. While it gives an inherent strength to survive, it also handicaps them by burdening them with heavy restriction. The notion that women are basically inferior to men is instilled into them from the start, giving them a mindset which they find difficult to discard. Subsequently, Saru, in *The Dark Holds No Terrors*, resents the greater love and attention given to her brother, Dhruv, in her parental home. Jaya, in *That Long Silence*, also refers to her elder brother, Dinu, ironically as "Ai's son," (41) the one to whom her mother was most attentive, while she was ignored. And though he did not need the Bombay flat, since he was settled abroad, it was he who got it from Ai. Jaya had been resentful and got hurt when she heard about it. Jaya frankly says referring to her mother's gift to Dinu. Moreover, her relatives make her feel that she does not belong to her parental home. When her uncle, Ramukaka, gets a family tree prepared, she is nowhere there in it. When she enquires, she is told: "You don't belong to this family! You're married; you're now part of Mohan's family. You have no place here."[10] It clearly puts a question mark on the sense of belongingness. It can be easily extracted from above that woman's place is nowhere. It is neither in her parental home nor in her husband's house. Quest of identity prevails, too, in Jaya's character. *That Long Silence*, though mainly concerned with Mohan, Jaya and the impending disaster, affords glimpse of mother and grandmothers. Jaya dislikes her mother and has contempt for her slapdash ways. She blames her equally for not preparing her for the duties of a woman's life. She expresses her anger in no uncertain terms. She is aware of the sense of right or wrong. Why are you late? Who was that you were talking to? Where are you going now? Jaya is not ready to listen anything. Why these questions are always asked to girls? Whereas on the other hand it is not so with a male child. The roots of gender discrimination can easily be perceived in this novel too. Like the protagonists of the other novels, Jaya has a stormy relationship with Ai who, like most traditional women, showers her affection upon her sons while neglecting her daughter. It creates seclusion in the life of a daughter. Like Sarita, Jaya tries to be as dissimilar from her mother as possible, rejecting her totally as a role-model. Jaya says that she knows what is good for her and what is not, she is no more a kid. Jaya's memories of her two grandmothers, the Ajji and the other – Ajji, are not complimentary either. The other-Ajji was a terrible mother and Ajji was no exception to it. Other-Ajji guards her position of power jealously, so much so that distrust and animosity have become deep rooted in her. She dislikes giving up her power even as she lies dying, regarding everybody as potential rival. The two grandmothers represent an aspect of the traditional Indian woman. Both women dominate their families, but with a difference. Overtly their attitudes may differ, but in many ways, both are responsible for hindering their children's growth and evolution. The perspective is entirely Jaya's and therefore one-sided, nonetheless, the fact remains that she viewed her grandmothers as powerful women.

## 2.2. Hostility Between Parents

Shashi Deshpande's woman is not merely educated; she is a co-breadwinner and extends her husband's income to maintain the standard of living they aspire to provide for their children. Thus, she has assumed a new role for herself in the wake of changed circumstances. This has, however, not exempt her from her traditional role and responsibility in the family which, in addition to her career-consciousness, has led to severe problems of adjustment. It is the main cause of her agony today. As shown in the character of Vanaa's daughter, Mandira. She is a perfect example of how people in general grow up with pre-conceived notions of the role of a woman as a mother and as a wife. Mandira apparently thinks that a woman's first duty is to look after her home and children. She gets hurt from the fact that her mother leaves her and her sister in the care of maid servant. Children feel neglected in the absence of the mother from home. The roots of seclusion and isolation start growing among them which compel them to revolt. This comes out as a consequence of non-communication between mother and the child. Mandira, a secluded child in *The Binding Vine*, dislikes working mothers. Again and again, she says that when she grows up, she would never leave her children alone because she herself dislikes being left to the care of a maidservant. Y.S. Sunita Reddy specifies, "one reads the recurring sagas of mothers over generation, enduring almost identical lifestyles. It is evident that the idea of the mother being solely responsible for taking care of the children has remained unchanged."[11] But the question arises as to why the woman being solely responsible for a child's care? No one dares to ask anything to man. The conflict between Urmila and her mother Inni is direct and straight forward and is the greatest example of the same. Urmi's hostility towards her mother is felt in the angry tone and harsh language she uses when speaking with her or about her to others. It shows the thanklessness of the child. The devious manner of rejecting her mother suggests the deep antagonism in Urmila towards her mother. As a child, Urmi had been sent away to Ranidurg to be looked after by her grandparents. Somehow, she had perceived this action as indicative of her mother's rejection of her and developed a deep resentment and anger in her against her mother. There is the lack of communication in mother-daughter relationship which creates the dilemma of seclusion in the life of the daughter. Consequently she develops a kind of hatred and rejection for her mother. Though a grown-up woman now and a mother herself, Urmi had never asked Inni why she had sent her away and had continued to assume that it had been her mother's decision. Although this is not the reality, even her brother Amrut, tells her that her father had been a domineering person who brooked no challenge to his decisions, Urmi conveniently ignores the information and continues to hold her mother responsible for the separation. She is aggressive and unassertive towards her mother. Urmi callously rejects Inni's solicitousness towards her after the death of her baby daughter Anu. She is not ready to share her grief with her own mother. The hostility is proved when Urmi told Vanna that as a child she had preferred the old-fashioned, ill-fitting dresses made for her by Baiajji, her grandmother, to the expensive ones sent by Inni. She would keep the dresses sent by her mother in the cupboard. It shows the thanklessness of the child. Even without asking for the reason of her sending away, Urmi declares Inni the sole cause of her seclusion. There are several situations in the novel when Urmi accuses her mother for not teaching her the manner of managing the house. The perspective is Urmila's. Hidden in this accusation is the patriarchal charge that Inni was not a perfect mother and housemaker for she had preferred her daughter to manage the house for her to the other way round.

Shashi Deshpande's novels generally centre on family relationships. Aru (Arundhati), the eldest daughter of Sumi and Gopal in *A Matter of Time*, does not allow her father to go "scot-free" [(MT, pp.137)]. Gopal walks out on his parental responsibilities. The daughters Aru, Charu and Seema feel secluded and lonely because of their father's absence from the house. Aru is the focal point to the novelist in the novel. She is a keen observer of the drama affecting the entire family. She seems to be holding a moral scale against which she would measure everyone including herself. Her concern makes her the most sensitive character in the novel that silently reaches out to others and feels their predicament keenly. Another distinguishing quality of Aru is her rebelliousness. She rebels against her father. Gopal's walking away on his family very much affected her. She cannot understand her father's desertion, her mother's apparent indifference or the oppressive silence between her grandparents. She feels deeply cloistered and secluded. She cannot find the reasons of her father's desertion. The desire to rebel is deeply ingrained in her. Gopal's walking away on his family, according to her, is not just a tragedy; it is both a shame and disgrace. Her reaction to her mother's stoic acceptance of it is violent and sharp. The pitiable condition of her mother and sisters encouraged her to revolt against her father who is the only person responsible for all the problems. The desire to rebel is her hostility; it is like a weapon of an antagonist. Her searching question makes Gopal re-examine his motives in fleeing from the family. She will not let him go scot-free. She is pained, frustrated and disappointed by his separation of the family, but her self-respect would not let her stoop to self-pity. She approaches Gopal not expecting sympathy for her or for her mother but unravel the strange behaviour of her father.

## 2.3. Extra-Marital Interest on the Part of A Parent

Madhu, in *Small Remedies,* has only a father, being a motherless child. She has been brought up by her freedom-loving father and a male servant, Babu. She is able to relate well to his father and to other surrogate fathers like Joe and Hamidbhai. Even relationship with father is difficult in societies where gender seclusion is accepted, and the young growing girl is advised to give up both free movement and free communication. But it sits easier than motherhood on the individual because a man does not have to struggle for an independent identity. The mysteries of being a female have been brought home to her by a childhood friend, Munni, who is the daughter of Savitribai Indorekar and her table player, Ghulam Saab. Both Munni's and Madhu's families are unusual. Madhu is gently possessive of her father and is shocked by the idea of his having a mistress. Her mother was her father's second wife and having lost two wives in close succession, he abandons the idea of marriage. Savitribai, on the other hand, is married into a respectable family, but her passion for music has led her to break away from its confines and to build up a life of her own. Munni is the daughter of Savitribai's relationship with her tabla player. Was he her lover or simply a man who could protect her? But Munni's whole effort is spent in rejecting this paternity and in breaking away from her life. She hates her mother. The hatred and rejection is so much that later, both the mother and daughter wipe out each other from their lives. Munni refuses to recognise even Madhu when they meet in a bus and Savitribai suppresses to mention her when she is being interviewed for her biography. Madhu certainly did not ask for the silence Savitribai exercises with respect to Munni. It was as if Munni does not exist. It was as if those years when Munni and Madhu were neighbours in Neemgaon where Madhu's father was a doctor, did not happen. All those years ago in Neemgaon, Madhu could not comprehend why Munni so disliked her father, the tabla-player, Ghulam Ahmed with whom Savitribai was living. Munni is the child of this union, a child who rejects her father and later she is disowned by her mother. The girl rejected her famous mother and took the name Shailaja Joshi, died by a strange coincidence, like Adit on the same day. Both were the victims of the same madness that gripped the country in the aftermath of the Babri Masjid incident in Ayodhya.

Sunita Reddy says: "Shashi Deshpande spares no effort to present the picture of life it is without conforming to stereotypes. This is more obvious in her portrayal of motherhood, which she seldom glorifies."[(Reddy, pp. 131)] Her protagonist, Madhu accepts that in movies the mother always appears as glorified figure but in reality, it is entirely different. In this fast-paced world the mother is like Munni's mother who is very selfish and stern. She ignored her daughter and almost vanish her existence from her life. But in all these relationships, emotional backgrounds are very important. Childhood experiences and memories go a long way towards moulding life, attitude, and personal relationships. The feeling of rejection, a traumatic memory, tension in the household, sexual discrimination, extramarital interest on the part of a parent, all these things influence future relationships. Naren in *Roots and Shadows* is an unwanted distant kin and this feeling of not having any anchorage at all becomes, in the end, the cause for his suicide. Mohan in *That Long Silence,* had a deprived childhood. As a child, he had refused to accompany his siblings to the charity dinners where his mother had been called to help. According to Jasbir Jain, "he had always found it difficult to be servile and humble, to be ignored or shoved into a corner."[12] This gives him a class complex and guides his choice of partner. It also defines his notion of right and wrong as well as of respectability. Gopal's condemnation of his mother's second marriage *A Matter of Time,* is clearly evident from his actions. Gopal, when he learns that his father is the second husband of his mother, begins to trace in it a betrayal to her first marriage. It dislocates him and pushes his life into a place of insecurity and cautiousness, distrustful of the future. Other parent-child relationships, which have had a lasting impact, are Leela's relationship with her mother in *Small Remedies,* and Urmi's with her mother Inni in *The Binding Vine*. Leela, like Mira in *The Binding Vine*, is given away in marriage much against her own wishes, but unlike Mira, she is encouraged to find herself in the world outside. Vasant is not the kind of possessive husband who wishes only to satisfy his desire. Urmi has always felt distant from her mother Inni and escaping a generation she has attached herself to her grandmother. Inni is the submissive wife who has failed to take a stand against the punishment which took away her daughter from her. Inni is seen as a mother who lacks the maternal instinct and still wants to look young and go out and have a life outside the restriction of domesticity.

The mother-daughter antagonism experienced by Saru and her mother in *The Dark Holds No Terrors*, is reflected by Mrs. Raman and her daughter in *Come Up And Be Dead.* The novel contains with in it several ideas in a converted form, ideas which Shashi Deshpande developed in her later novels. Manjari in *Moving On*, feels a kind of betrayal or the sense of complete seclusion. Her mother Mai always showers her love towards her younger daughter Malu, and not to Manjari (jiji). Although Jiji, herself loves Malu and Mai both, but "she knows the truth that she has to work harder."[13 (MO, pp.44)] if she wanted to be loved by the mother. The mother becomes impossible when Jiji wants to get married with Shyam, the man according to her choice. She refuses the offer and says that Jiji's love for Shyam was nothing but merely a physical passion. She never tries to understand the inner feeling of her own daughter. There is lack of communication between them. Like Saru and Indu, Jiji also revolts against Mai and marries to Shyam. This creates a rift between them. When Malu became pregnant, the mother blames Jiji for that. She says that it was Jiji's fault. She was the guilty person, she was the wrongdoer. But it was Shyam who had made Malu pregnant. After that the life of Jiji was totally changed.

## 2.4. Fathers Are More Supportive Than Mothers

Another aspect of parent-child relationship is the relationship of daughters to their fathers. This relationship is also projected at several levels. Shashi Deshpande has stated that conflicts between mothers and daughters are natural. The daughter in a traditional family is considered the responsibility of the mother who imposes restrictions on her to prepare for a harsher future as part of the process of socialisation. Fathers are perceived as lenient towards daughters who feel oppressed by their mother's strictures. The patriarchies of the fathers remain hidden as the women act on their behalf to condition the daughter. The conflict between mother daughter relationships is direct. It is reflected in almost all the mother-daughter relationships in the work of Shashi Deshpande. Sarita's father is an easy-going, traditional, non-interfering type of person who leaves the upbringing of his children to his wife, who dominates the household. Like most conservative fathers, he has kept his distance from Sarita. He rarely took any interest in her school and college and left it all to her mother. He had always been incapable of strong feelings. He is concerned only with that which his wife asked him to do. The distance between Sarita and her father had increased when her brother Dhruv died accidentally. Sarita got hurt at her father's lack of demonstration of affection towards her and believes that he is a weak man who had allowed himself to be dominated by his wife. However, despite his traditional background, he had supported Sarita against his wife in a few crucial situations. Among these, the most important had been his encouragement to Sarita in her wish to join a medical college in Bombay. This decision forcefully had proved to be a turning point in her life. While her mother had violently opposed Sarita's ambition of becoming a doctor, since it would be difficult to marry off an overqualified girl, her father had stood by her firmly. Out of his meager salary, he had paid for her education and enabled her to realise her ambition. Later, when Sarita tells him about Manu's nightmare, he listens carefully and patiently to outpouring. Despite his traditional outlook, he urges her to talk to Manu about the problem. He advises her not to run away from Manu. It is the sign of cowardice. He tells her that she had been wrong to hide Manu's physical brutality from him. She ought to have talked to Manu about it and tried to find a solution to the problem, instead of avoiding it. The unexpected blame, accusation from her father, makes her realise that the duty to set things right was upon her and that she would have to act in an assertive manner to resolve the conflict. Sarita's father thus proves to be an important force in Sarita's evolution. Though he had always remained in the background, preferring his wife to take the lead, he had supported Saru at all crucial moments in her life. Although he is a typical Indian father-old fashioned, conservative, and reserved with his daughter but had always tried to understand her problems and motivated her to solve them. This relationship works towards an equal relationship. The father had supported her demand to be educated. Indu's and Jaya's fathers in *Roots and Shadows* and *That Long Silence*, respectively are modern and broad-minded and remarkably free of the patriarchal ideology. Their attitudes and values play an important role in shaping their daughter's personalities. Although portrayed somewhat skilfully, they are seen as having influenced their daughters in becoming independent women. Gopal in *A Matter of Time* walks out on his paternal responsibilities, but Sumi towards the end is able to work out a kind of relationship with her own father. Madhu in *Small Remedies,* had only a father, being a motherless child and she is able to relate well to him and to other surrogate fathers like Joe and Hamidbhai. Even father's attitude is difficult in societies where gender segregation is accepted, and the young growing girl is advised to give up both free movement and free communication. Indu's father is a widower and a journalist. As a journalist, he had to travel; so Indu was reared by his brother's family. Indu's attitude towards her father is quite unambiguous. In her joint family, she had many surrogate fathers like Kaka and Old Uncle, so she had never missed her father. Yet at one time when he had played a very important role in her life, was when he had insisted that she attend an English-medium school, unlike her cousins who used to go to a vernacular medium school. The training had set her apart from her cousins and given Indu the necessary head start in life. Later, like her father, she chooses to be a free-lance Journalist. She had been influenced by his intellectual, ethical, moral and social values, though her later submission to Jayant's wishes seems to threaten those very values. During her visit to the old house, she realises her own weakness in having granted to Jayant's demand that she compromises her writing. Her father had never compromised his ideals and values. Her quest for self-identity ends in her resolve to be honest to herself, like her father. Jaya's father in *That Long Silence*, also displays a supportive role towards his daughter which inspires her growth as an individual. He is quite unconventional for a man of his generation. He had married for love, out of his community and flouted custom by shifting out of the ancestral home with his bride. This had been a major step for him, especially since he was his mother's favourite and in those days it was not customary to set up a nuclear family. To Jaya, in retrospect, this action seems to be a rebellion against the control that her grandmother exercised over her children. Jaya had been deeply attached to her father. Like all mothers, her mother had always shown preference for her sons, and Jaya had grown up resenting this attitude; but her father, unlike most traditional fathers, had always made up for her mother's indifference. Not only would he support her but he would also actually demonstrate his affection towards her. In most Indian families, the girl child is usually left to the care of her mother, the father rarely interferes in her upbringing or displaying his love for her openly. Jaya's father, on the other hand, would even encourage her short temper[TLS, pp.82], a trait considered unbecoming in a girl. Her western education (insisted upon by her father) had given her an unconservative outlook. He was proud that she was different from her cousins, "You are not like the others, Jaya," Appa had said to me, pulling me ruthlessly out of the safe circle in which the other girls had stood…." (TLS, pp.136) Jaya's father is the most feminist among the fathers in Shashi Deshpande's novels father is the most feminist among the fathers in Shashi Deshpande's novels. He had never displayed any kind of gender-bias towards his daughter. On the contrary, he had nurtured her to become an independent and individualistic person. His support and guidance are influential in developing Jaya's fundamental attitude and principles. Although he appears as a minor character in the novel, he is powerful in moulding her basic values and character.

The usual pattern in Shashi Deshpande's fiction has been a better daughter-father equation than a daughter-mother equation. This is true of Sarita, Indu and Jaya, and that is how it also seems initially in *The Binding Vine*, too. Urmila respects her father and resents her mother whom she holds responsible for sending her away to Ranidurg to be brought up by her grandparents. Seen through Urmila's eyes, her father is projected as advisable and firm, and she admires him much. It is Amrut, her younger brother (who had been brought up in his natal home), who corrects her perspective. From Amrut she learns that her father was a patriarchal, authoritarian person: "I always thought Papa was brutal, No Amrut, that's too harsh! Why? Do you think you have to use physical violence to be brutal? Even to force you will on another is to be brutal…."[14]. This revelation adds a new dimension to the marital power relationship. A man may love his wife, as Urmila's father loved her mother, and yet deny her voice so completely as to cause untold mental torture and suffering. Urmila recalls how, when her father was deadly ill, he had expressed deep-felt remorse at having sent her away for Kartik's delivery at Ranidurg to her in law's home. Urmi does not understand the full import of his words until many years later, when her mother tells her how mercilessly he had forced Inni to send her to look after by his parents. The incident had been traumatic both for Urmila who felt rejected and for Inni who had been made to feel she was a bad mother. Urmi who had always thought of her father as a wise man, is shocked at the unwitting cruelty and the injustice of his act towards Inni and realises how much her father had wronged her mother by imposing his rigid will on her. Thus, in a way different from the fathers of the other protagonists, Urmi's father also is a contrast to Kishore. While her father was a domineering and patriarchal husband and father, Kishore is a modern, liberated husband and parent.

In the novels of Shashi Deshpande, fathers appear to be more accessible and approachable. Savitribai in *Small Remedies* speaks warmly of her father despite the fact that he was the one major obstruction in her pursuit of music; Lata in the same novel thinks of her father while there is not a single photograph of her mother in the house. Sons on the other hand are resistant to their fathers and if not resistant, they distance themselves. For Mohan in *That Long Silence,* it is his father who is responsible for the kind of life they have led. Mohan's father is an intelligible example for the oppression and domination that characterise patriarchy. His cruelty to his wife and children symbolises the worst aspects of patriarchy. He is one of those men who believe that the man of the house is like a divine hero, while his wife is his property, a slave whose body is meant for physical gratification. Mohan's mother goes through several pregnancies which reduce her body to a skeleton. The above references reveal the traditionally superior position of the father, and the wife's considerably lower status. It also deconstructs and subverts the myth that the father is the head of the family and a protector of his wife. The relationships, in fact, respond negatively to the authority exercised by the same sex parent. Some forces like emotions, sibling jealousy and gender discrimination are equally responsible for filial ingratitude.

## Notes and References


1. Rashmi Sahi. "Mother-Daughter Relationship in The Novels Of Shashi Deshpande", *Indian English Literature:* Vol.II, ed. by Basavaraj Naikar, (New Delhi: Atlantic Publishers and Distributers, 2002), 131, here after cited in the chapter.
2. Usha Bande. *Mothers and Mother-Figures in Indo-English Literature,* (Jalandhar: ABS Publications, 1994), 134.
3. Shubha Tiwari. "The Heroine in The Dark Holds No Terrors by Shashi Deshpande", ed. by Amar Nath Prasad, *Indian Women Novelists In English,* (New Delhi: Atlantic Publishers and Distributors, 2001), 86.
4. Shashi Deshpande. *The Dark Holds No Terrors,* (New Delhi: Penguin Books, 1990), 63, here after cited in the chapter.
5. S. Anandalakshmi. "The Female Child in A Family Setting," *The Indian Journal Of Social Work,* Vol.LII, No.1, January 1991, 31.

6. Premila Paul. "The Dark Holds No Terrors; A Woman's Search for Refuge," *Indian Women Novelists in English*, Set I, Vol. V, ed. by R.K. Dhawan, (New Delhi: Prestige, 1991), 67.
7. Suman Bala. *Woman In the Novels of Shashi Deshpande*, (New Delhi: Khosla Publishing House, 2001), 69.
8. R.S. Pathak. *The Fiction of Shashi Deshpande*, (New Delhi: Creative Books, 1998), 35.
9. Shashi Deshpande. *Roots and Shadows,* (Hyderabad: Disha Books, 1992), 74. here after cited in the chapter.
10. Shashi Deshpande. *That Long Silence,* (London: Virgo Press, 1988), 143, here after cited in the chapter.
11. Y.S. Sunita Reddy. *A Feminist Perspective on The Novels of Shashi Deshpande,* (New Delhi: Prestige Books, 2001), 102, here after cited in the chapter.
12. Jasbir Jain. *Gendered Realities, Human Spaces: The Writing of Shashi Deshpande,* (Jaipur: Rawat Publication, 2003), 88-89.
13. Shashi Deshpande. *Small Remedies,* (New Delhi: Viking, Penguin 2000), 44, here after cited in the chapter.
14. Shashi Deshpande. *The Binding Vine,* (New Delhi: Penguin Books, 1993), 133, here after cited in the chapter.

## CHAPTER 3

# The Hollowness of Man Woman Relationship

Shashi Deshpande, in her novels specifies the unequal relationship existing between man and woman. The relation between man-woman is never taken to be a relation among two equals. Woman is a non-entity and that has to be her fate. Whatever identity she is supposed to have is conferred on her by man. She is like a slave and man is like a master. A slave does not have his or her own wish, similarly woman cannot act according to her wish, but she has to follow the duties that are prescribed by man. The moral code of conduct, which is almost followed religiously, looks upon woman as property. The individual self, whether man or woman, finds it constrained by the need to keep up appearances, to continue with the idea of pretence, for surfaces tend to hide rather than express. Somewhere there is the feeling that love is the expression of an ego, which expects total acceptance. Marriage is not a plain and simple contract, but it is a part of a larger human relationship, which passes through attraction, love, physical relationships, living together and a whole lot of other phases such as parenthood. The two people who get married do not lose or dissolve their identity, they remain two individual human beings and thus seclusion, disappointment and disagreement do fall to their lot. Shashi Deshpande asks the question: Why do people get married? Man and woman opt for matrimony for very different reasons, reasons that are culturally governed. When they work at a personal level, then, too, there are psychological differences. This relationship in Indian context has gained considerable hallowedness. Thus, married woman is given importance and treated respectfully. The qualities of piousness, chastity and generosity are thrust on her, and married woman is expected to imitate the role of a silent and faithful wife. A girl child in India is brought up with the view that she is to be ultimately married. Many Indo-Anglian woman novelists delineate seclusion experienced by woman after marriage. Shashi Deshpande also explores in great psychological depth the oppression of woman by patriarchal society and woman's own complicity in her oppression. Her novels capture middle class Hindu woman's daily emotional battles with great vividness. Her novels present a social world of many complex relationships, many men and women live together and journey across life in their different age groups, classes, and gendered roles. Doubt, anxiety and often a feeling of void of values push characters in her novels to intense self-examination. Woman is particularly caught in the process of redefining and rediscovering her own role, position, and relationships with in her given social world.

## 3.1 Marriage without Emotional Involvement

Marriage locates itself in romance, sexuality, and social environment. Several marriages in the novels of Shashi Deshpande are built around the initial doctrine of attraction and in themselves symbolise a rebellion on the part of woman. Few of them are across caste lines and result in long-term breaches with the parental family. In arranged marriages, arranged on whatever grounds, and also in love marriages, sexuality has its own role to play. Love, acceptance, response, yielding or withdrawal, frigidity, aversion and self-hatred, in some degree, all come to rest on the point of physical relationships with in or without marriage. Even the struggle between the claims of freedom and the claims of the body come to rest on this. According to Jasbir Jain, "Man-woman relationships, marriages and estrangements are a central concern with Shashi Deshpande in novel after novel as she moves from the marriage of acceptance to other relationships that fall outside parent controlled contracts."[1] Several of her woman characters question the idea of romance as it has been culturally inherited by them, test its strength and limit against their social reality and explore its meaning through a physical relationship. The struggle, both at the personal level and the social level, is between the body and the mind. In an arranged marriage, they may often be at odds, and even in a love relationship, they may not find an equal recognition. Infact all courtships and attractions are looked upon retrospectively. It is hardly ever that a relationship is projected in its initial phases. Functioning along with fixed parameters, marriages become an arid formality, devoid of contact. Shashi Deshpande often presents in her novels the references of woman's seclusion suggested through the images of dust, barrenness, and dark room. It creates hollowness within relationship. The hollowness of man woman relationship is based on socially predetermined patterns of gender inequality. In the women characters, seclusion takes an intensity and sharpness through the added frustration of being marginalised. These hyper-sensitive women have their material wants taken care of but their emotional needs cry desperately to be acknowledged. According to Jasbir Jain, "The reasons of their loneliness lie in the gap between the romantic idea of surrender and the reality of separateness; the conflict is between their individuality and their emotional need to be absorbed." (J.J. pp.85) Marriage does not have the same relevance to man as to a woman. The two persons are different from each other, though one has the necessity of the other. Marriage subjugates and enslaves woman.

A direct juxtaposition of the romantic idea of marriage and the realistic attack on it is worked out through the character of Manu in *The Dark Holds No Terrors.* This novel tells the story of a marriage on the rocks. Manu (Manohar) is the romantic lover of Saru (Sarita) who has married with him against her parents' wishes. Infact the marriage has secluded her from them for several years. Finally, she comes home after the death of her mother, who had died without extending any forgiveness or making any gestures of reconciliation. Saru's marriage to Manu is a means of that love and security which she had always lacked in life. She marries to secure the lost love in her parental home and her identity as individual. As S.P. Swain writes: "her marriage with Manu is an assertion on and affirmation of her feminine sensibility."[2] He is the ideal romantic hero who has come to rescue her from the insecure, loveless existence. Manu is a lecturer of English literature, a young man who as a student was one of the known names. There had been an aura of distinction about him, as a good student, a budding writer, a poet of promise, secretary of Literary Association, actively involved in debating society and the life and soul of dramatics society. They had had their groups of friends-budding poets and writers full of enthusiasm and aspiring dreams. She enjoyed their company. Manu also showed her off as his doctor wife. But soon she wanted to get along in life. She was not satisfied with her small hospital salary and Manu's uncertain income as journalist. The idea of an unemployed husband seemed a horrible humiliation. She insisted that Manu must have a regular job and was happy when he managed to get the job of a lecturer in a private college. Manu protested; it would stifle his aspirations. But to Saru, 'her husband teaches in a college', sounded more respectable than 'her husband is a journalist'. Ultimately both were caught in the money web. Manu's quiet acceptance of her action got her annoyed and when he did not question the patron's offer of finance to help Saru to start a private practice, her annoyance turned into despise. At the same time, her marriage begins to crumble under the burden of success in her profession. She is happy until she begins to establish herself as a doctor. Now the situation undergoes a change. Till now, "he had been the young man and I, his bride. Now I was the lady doctor, and he was my husband."[3] When Saru had got married she had sworn that she would never dominate over her husband because there is something about female domination which ultimately destroys the man. It baffled her to find that she had actually resulted in doing that which she had sworn never to do and destroyed Manu's manhood. She had actually murdered him. It hurts him to be pushed into a corner of insignificance and he reacts by becoming overaggressive so that she shudders at the very thought of his touch. Manu, her husband, cannot tolerate that people greet her and ignore him. He begins to get rough and abrupt with her in love-making. The second disrupting incident happens when a girl, interviewing her for a women's magazine, ask Manohar, "how does it feel when your wife earns not only the butter but most of the bread as well"? (DHNT, pp.200) Manohar turns an animal at night and attacks Sarita. Thus begin her nightmares. Saru's animus is stultified when he sadistically rapes her whenever he wishes to salvage his ego. She starts hating the man-woman relationship which is based on attraction and need, not on love. Saru says, "love.... how she scorned the word now. There was no such thing between man and woman. There was only a need which both fought against, futilely....... turning into the thing they called "love". It's only a word she thought. Take away the word, the idea, and the concept will wither away." (DHNT, pp.72) This is an awkward situation in which she is placed. At a personal level, she feels a gradual disappearance of love and attachment, which she had once developed. It is now replaced by a psychological conflict which is uncalled for but inevitable, given the situation in which both of them have been placed. Most of her solemn duties towards her husband and children are unattended too. Her status in society rises day by day while there is a decline in her conjugal relationship. It may imply at one level that her rise in importance is inversely proportionate to the fall in the importance of her husband, creating a conflict between her achieved position and the ascribed position of Manu. She reasons thus: "It is because I am something more than his wife that he has become what he is." (DHNT, pp.78) This note of self-accusation is indicative of her growing up to be a woman in the quietness of her parental home. This novel is about the quest of an anxious, eager, ambitious, self-assertive, and self-righteous woman, Sarita who gains her identity successfully. The individual in Saru is in crisis on all fronts-as a mother, a wife, a sister, a daughter, and above all an Indian woman. The novelist's analysis of her character brings out the real problem of our view. Saru's personality is continually being eroded by the fact that she is merely a girl. Once she fails to fulfill the eternal female dream of finding happiness through a man, she feels lost. It is as though the very purpose of her breathing is gone-she has failed to please her man. Her fierce feminism is a reaction against this very unjust belief of society. She tells the girls bitterly, "A wife must always be a few feet behind her husband. .... That's the only rule to follow if you want a happy marriage. Don't ever try to reverse the doctor-nurse, executive-secretary, principal-teacher role." (DHNT, pp.137)

The point to ponder is that the concerned woman herself is not able to free herself from the duties of these social prejudices. One just cannot undo all the mental feeding one has received since one's birth. The vehemence evinced in the words quoted above makes one feel how strong the sense of injury has been in Saru's heart. But she herself is helplessly entangled in the racial and social prejudices prevalent. Saru is conscious of the fact that she is superior to her husband in her qualifications, social status, and mental caliber and in many other respects. But in her inner self, she rebels against it. The irony of fate is such that Manu allows her to lead the life of a simple housewife, not subordinate to his superior wisdom, nor does he tolerate her higher status. Not only Manu, but Saru also could not and would not accept it as a natural consequence of a mating which is rather extraordinary.

In *Roots and Shadows*, Indu too searches for release from the constraints of the traditional and tradition-bound institution of marriage in search of an autonomous self, only to realise like them, again, that this refuge is hard to achieve. In this novel, the focus is on Indu's family home. She also has a sense of discontentment and failure, haunting her where her husband is concerned. Marriage, too, is viewed critically and condemned as a euphemism for lust. Indu also envisages it as a tragic-comic picture of "a cage with two animals glaring hatred at each other."[4] Indu and Saru both try to find meaning in marriage and at the same time they try to retain their own individuality.

Shashi Deshpande's protagonists are trying to find solutions for the actualities. Highly sensitive, intelligent, and educated Indu could be said to be a representative of modern young women. She always aspires to become an independent and complete in herself. At the same time, she finds dominant Akkà and even the family to be a hindrance in achieving her goal of independence and completeness. Hating the suppression, she had to face in the family, she breaks away from it and marries Jayant: "I had felt incomplete, not as a woman, but as a person. And in Jayant I had thought I had found the other part of my whole self.[(RS, pp.67)] But she soon comes to realise that marriage makes one dependent.

In this novel, there is an immeasurable distance between the idea and the reality. Indu in her very first meeting with Jayant is swept off her feet. He gives her a feeling of solidity and certainty. She had thought that marriage would give her happiness and an identity of her own, but this does not happen. She realises that marriage, the promised land for every girl, is nothing but another trap. It is an enclosure which obstructs the movement towards autonomy and self-realisation. She says: "When I look in the mirror, I think of Jayant, when I dress, I think of Jayant… Always what he wants, what he would like, what would please him…? Have I become so fluid, with no shape? no form of my own."[(RS, pp.49)]

The paradox in Indu's life is that she loves Jayant. Yet she feels that in loving and marrying him she has lost a part of her real self. Her married life seems hypocritical. She does not reveal her real feelings before Jayant lest she may disappoint him. Her marriage with Jayant brings no satisfaction and happiness. It threatens to rob Indu of herself. It is because of Jayant, that Indu's life is both meaningful and meaningless. Indu wants to be a writer. She works as a journalist. But even Jayant expects her to do the stereotyped insincere work, the editor wants her to do, because he always says, 'we need the money.' Ultimately Indu feels that she has sacrificed her real self to please Jayant. Even professionally she has no satisfaction because she must follow the dictates of the editor and not conscience. Her marriage to Jayant has compelled in her a duality of life. As a result of her unhappy conjugal life with Jayant, she enters a physical relationship with Naren. But Indu does not see what she has done with Naren is wrong. She thinks it to be no crime or sin to make love with another person besides her husband, but this feeling is, short lived. Later, she feels that she has cheated Jayant and her relationship with Naren is dishonourable and dishonest. Jayant could never accept that a woman can have sexual desires. Therefore' Indu had always held back. Now she realises that each time she had cut off some part of her real self to please Jayant, but this had turned their marriage into a farce. Indu tries hard to find reasons for the unhappiness in her married life and comes to the conclusion that self-surrenders and self-abnegation are her greatest enemies. She feels that she loves her husband passionately whereas Jayant never tries to understand what she really wants or feels; there is obviously a lack of communication between them.

Shashi Deshpande's earlier novels focus on one protagonist and one central man-woman relationship. Her novel *The Binding Vine,* has a much more complex structure. It explores many possible variations on the theme, by portraying different couples having different power equations, established between them. The central character of the novel is Urmila, an English lecturer, married to Kishore, who is the boy next-door, whom she had known and played in childhood. She had fallen in love with him and had finally married with the full consent of both families. Yet Urmi's relationship with Kishore is far from perfect. She walks out of the bedroom and her husband's house on her wedding night because she saw the fear and the trapped look on his face when he said flippantly, "The two of us in a closed room and we can't get out. That's marriage."[5] It is perhaps because she wants to prove that their marriage at least is not a trap with any escape, but a relationship in which each individual retains the option of independent action that she does so. The next morning, he just walks through the hedge separating their houses as casually as he had always done. He has tea with her family and then they both walk back to his house. There are no recriminations and no explanations. But the memory of the closed look she had seen on his face on their wedding night, remains with her. It makes it impossible for her to speak with him freely of her innermost feelings. She knows that "Kishore will never remove his armour, there is something in him I will never reach"(BV, pp.141) and as long as he is afraid of letting himself go, of baring his soul to another's gaze, their relationship would always be less than perfect. There is no communication between them. Due to this non-communication, Urmi feels secluded. Kishore is neither spontaneous nor emotional like her. He is totally different in nature. He is in the Merchant Navy, and so stays away for long stretches of time. This distance creates a huge space in their relationship. After the death of their baby daughter, Anu, Kishore had become absolutely uncommunicative. The death of Anu acts as a catalyst, and Urmi is compelled to re-define her relationship with Kishore.

Another protagonist Madhu in *Small Remedies,* too, suffers in her relationship with her husband. She leaves home partly to cope with her bereavement and partly to get away from her husband, Som. Her relationship with Som has been a strained one, ever since he learnt of her premarital attraction. The tension between husband and wife has driven their son, Aditya, first out of the house, and then, out of this world. Several man-woman relationships are projected in the novel. Out of these, there are three that deserve detailed analyses-Som-Madhu, Joe-Leela and Savitribai-Ghulam Saab relationships. Each is very different from the other as is a fourth one, that of Madhu's host and hostess, Lata and Hari, which is also very unusual with both having their freedom and yet belonging together. The relationship of Joe-Leela, is an older version of this, where across religion and language they have built a lovely relationship, supportive of each other and with enough space for both idealism and activism. In both in these relationships there is respect for each other, and they recognise the need for personal space. Contrasted with them, the other two relationships are power relationships. Savitribai has used Ghulam Saab for her own ends. In her relationship with Ghulam Saab, she has a daughter Munni. Savitribai's obsession with her profession is an all absorbing one and leaves no space for emotions. As far as Madhu is concerned, it is a case of a normal young woman who loves life and marries Som on the basis of an attraction. Having missed a family life, she now wants a family. She values human relationships. She is not at all gender conscious and is comfortable in both worlds. She says, "Brought up by a father, I never felt the strangeness, the otherness of men myself, nor did I feel the need to be part of a female group… "[6] But marriage views gender neutrality with suspicion. A series of grief-causing incidents are narrated in the novel to show how these have been compressed in the unconscious plane of Madhu's character. The past is also intruded into the present, causing havoc in Madhu's married life. Shashi Deshpande explores the repercussions of these events and the feelings of grief, guilt and remorse, overwhelm the character. One particular incident that had happened many years ago in Madhu' early girlhood on the day she received the tragic news of her beloved father's death is significant. When Madhu had been reeling under the shock of her father's death, a man trusted to be her father's friend had entered her room to comfort her. As he touched her comfortingly, he had been overcome by passion and had taken advantage of Madhu's vulnerable position and her innocent body. Madhu impulsively speaks to Som about this physical incident of the past. She explains that she did not speak of this incident to him because it had been lost to her memory after her father's death. For Madhu it was neither real nor a part of her life. It was always like a dream. However, for Som, it is a shattering revelation. Their whole married relationship seems to be hinged on this truth which has its root in cultural tradition, and has led to the heightened value, attached to purity and chastity. This discovery of Madhu's past freezes Som's feelings towards his wife. He refuses to recognise her as the woman who has shared her life with him. He secludes himself from his wife and keeps himself alone. A change begins to set in their relationship. Although Som tries to behave as though nothing is different, but he ceases even to touch her. He is careful not to make any physical contact with her. Slowly he becomes possessed of the thought that she is not completely his own. Unable to accept the idea that his wife is not the woman as he imagined before the marriage, he reacts violently. In course of time, Madhu finds the torture endless as Som brings up the names of all those, he imagined could have been her lovers. Thus, Madhu is filled with helpless rage and turns on him in fury but she also feels an enormous grief under his suspicion and anger. Madhu no longer replies to him. However, she understands that her silence, "makes things worse, it's a bigger barrier between us than my words had been." (SR, 256) When Som secludes himself from his wife, Madhu thinks of going away but she wonders where she could go and how she could leave her son, Adit. Thus, Som and Madhu are locked in silent and fearful struggle that exhausts both of them. Unfortunately for both of them it is on one of those days when they are quarreling that Adit comes and finds them struggling together. His parents shout at him to go away as they do not want him involved in their own anguish. That day the post-independence riots are especially severe and Adit never returns as he is killed in a bomb blast. Madhu is now doubly secluded, both physically and emotionally from her son as well as her husband. Now, Madhu must face the most terrible grief along with her broken relationship with Som. Under the circumstances, Madhu and Som can draw no comfort from each other. They fight with their grief separately, each filled with guilt. According to them it was their quarrel that had driven Aditya away, into the arms of danger and death. The days that follow Aditya's death, are full of anguish and filled with an agony that Madhu can barely endure. Hence, when Madhu accepts the job of writing the life of Savitribai, Som is glad that she is going away for a while, and he is to be alone to sort out his own confused state. Like Madhu, who is suffocated by grief, Som also feels the need to recover his balance, to cope with the conflicting emotions that refuse to calm down. At the moment he cannot face his wife and longs to be apart, to be alone. He too, needs inner space to think, to be with himself. For Madhu, it is an attempt to emancipate herself from her grief. In this novel, the novelist analyses the protagonist's conflicting thoughts on her husband's rejection and misunderstanding. Ranjini Singh gives her opinion that "the novelist also describes the suffering, distress and seclusion that Madhu undergoes before she is reconciled to her grief and once again establishes a place for herself in society as Som's wife and, above all, as a human being,"[7] The reason of the hollowness in man-woman relationship is the gap which lies between the romantic idea of surrender and the reality of separateness. The conflict is between their individuality and their emotional need to be absorbed.

In *If I Die Today*, as in Shashi Deshpande's other novels, one of the concerns of the novelist is to depict what happens to woman after marriage. What they have been, what they have become, and what is in store for them. On the surface, all is well with her middle-class women. They have a happy married life with their husbands and are blessed with children in most cases. Yet, there is something terrible in the state of their domestic and married life, for which to a considerable extent their spouses are somehow responsible. Education, economic independence, and motherhood are there to disturb the existing equation. The story of Manju and Vijay in *If I Die Today,* is a telling instance of it. In this kind of relationship neither the husband is an out and out bad sort, nor is the wife a clingy woman who sets out to be a victim. She has been a loving, affectionate understanding wife before she turned into an emotional pretzel. Now she is neither content nor confident. She is in a rather miserable state and unable to see that her feelings of misery are not due to her faults. She seems to have become a victim of a husband who neither hits the wife nor says even a single angry word to her, but by his actions, words and sly comments makes her feel guilt-ridden and censored. There is non-communication between them. Manju finds her married life fraught with silences and barriers. Even the second pregnancy which is supposed to bring husband and wife closer, fails to deliver the desired result. The wife being slowly silenced and distanced from her motherhood and finds her first daughter against her wishes growing up and clinging to her father like a vine. It seems that the motherhood is the cause of her misery, and it makes her feel like a breeding animal. The real problem, however, does not lie in womanhood, wifehood, or motherhood but in the attitude of the middle-class male which deprivileges the woman against the man, the moment she becomes a wife. Manju says, "A marriage. You start off expecting so many things. And bit by bit, like dead leaves, the expectations fall off. But… two people who have shut themselves off in two separate glass jar? Who can see each other but can't communicate? Is this a marriage?"[8]

## 3.2 Silences as the Strategy of Survival

There are some other man-woman relationships in the novels of Shashi Deshpande where silence is the strategy of survival. In *That Long Silence,* Jaya's married life becomes unbearable. A sense of non-fulfillment, of incompleteness had lain dormant in Jaya for years, suppressed out of fear of denting the façade of happy marriage. Her modern predicament and the flood of consciousness it generates in a silent stream. According to Jaya to strike a relationship, one has to learn a lot of tricks and, "Silence is one of them….. You never find a woman criticising her husband, even playfully, in case it might damage the relationship."[9] Jaya uncomplainingly, silently succumbs and surrenders to Mohan. She never says 'yes' when her husband asks her whether he has hurt her. She tolerates everything mutely. Male dominance and authority is represented through Mohan, Jaya's husband. A domineering husband and a suffering wife that is Jaya who does not immediately react to the situation, but the reader is insinuated through the flashback technique used by the author. A terrible feeling of guilt envelops her, but she remains helplessly passive. According to Sarla Palkar, "she perhaps does her role of wife to perfection but fails as a human being."[10] Through the character of

Jaya, Shashi Deshpande brilliantly portrays the seclusion of a woman living silently in a cage called marriage. The protagonist is meek, docile, submissive, and house-proud. She is the typical Indian housewife following her husband without any question, as his shadow. Siddhartha Sharma specifies that, "Shashi Deshpande's *That Long Silence,* is an expression of the silence of the modern Indian housewife. Although many women writers tried their hand at expressing this long silence that had turned woman into non-entities, they could only provide psychological depths to their characters."[11] She is a woman who adjusts and accommodates unlike the modern woman who finds herself and thus forced into the background by the claims of culture and hence adopt an inimical attitude towards it. Jaya's entire life is around her husband Mohan. This superficial contentment is shattered by a crisis. Mohan is accused of some malpractices and his friend advises him to lie low till the storm blows over. An enquiry is ordered, and Mohan immediately decides to leave his Church-gate flat and shift to a small shabby flat at Dadar and Jaya timidly follows him. It is here in this small Dadar flat Jaya starts discovering her. Her journey towards a well-defined selfhood is mired in the labyrinthine mazes of societal pressures, feminine conditioning to change oneself. According to the accepted norms of behaviour, suppressive and the continued dilemma of attaching a purpose to her life, culminates in a long silence. Y.S. Sunita Reddy delineates, "Shashi Deshpande unmasks both Jaya and Mohan when they face the crisis in their lives. They have run into stormy weather and their secure sheltered life washes away like a water colour in rainy storm."[12] Her silence is symptomatic of seclusion and apprehension rooted in every woman's soul in different forms – a silence which is often misunderstood by man as a symbol of woman's contentment. Jaya was aware of an inner void and the hollowness in her life, even though it was shielded by the deceptively beautiful screen of her social graces and obligations. There are moments when for Jaya, social and familial responsibilities do not remain a pleasure, but become a bondage, because she is forced to accept these compulsively as a female. Indira Bhatt observes, "Mohan wants to use his wife as buffer, an opiate to soften the impact of the forces he has set into motion against himself."[13] Her married life forces her to put herself on exhibition, but it does not enable her to understand herself successfully. Instead of taking her out of her seclusion, it confirms her alienation from the personal and the social worlds. As

Adele King in her book review says: "Jaya finds her normal routine so disrupted that for the first time she can look at her life and attempt to decide what she really is."[14] Her inability to establish a normal relationship with her husband enhances her frustration. Jaya, a name given by her father since her birth, was changed to Suhasini after her marriage. Mohan, her husband had given her that name. She became Suhasini and then marriage brought a change in Jaya's life. Jaya and Suhasini are two facets of the same coin, and these two collateral names of Shashi Deshpande's protagonist are symbolical in her social and familial import. Past disappointments flash-back across her mind. They enlighten the present. They portray the abounded and lonely Jaya's drift of thought and mood captured through the broken and fragmentary stream-of-consciousness; "A husband is like a sheltering tree, you have to keep the tree alive and flourishing, even if you have to water it with deceit and lies". (TLS, 32) Jaya's aunt had told her, leaving her to make the logical inferences that since the tree afforded shelter and protection. She often recalls the preaching that were thrust upon her when she was growing up. Marriage was the only career; Jaya had lost herself and become the male construct of an ideal wife. Veena Sheshadri writes: "One ends up by wondering whether Jaya has imposed the long silence on herself not out of a sense of duty or to emulate the ideal Hindu woman of the ages gone by, but in order to camouflage the streaks of ugliness with in her."[15] Jaya realises that it is not quarrels that shatter a marriage, it is doing things separately. Being aware for two years she would not be able to share her experiences with him. Each experience may act as a brick that can ultimately become a wall between them. She knows there is pain in hostility and anguish and agony in rebel and that is why she adopts a subaltern and subservient attitude: "No, what have I to do with these mythical women? I can't fool myself. The truth is simpler. Two bullocks yoked together.... It is more comfortable – for them to move in the same direction. To go in different directions would be painful, and what animal would voluntarily choose pain?" (TLS, 11-12)

Like Indu-Jayant, Saru-Manu, Jaya-Mohan and Urmi-Kishore, Sumi and Gopal in *A Matter of Time*, also enjoyed harmonious relationship during the early years of their marriage. Theirs too, is not the ordinary arranged marriage as Gopal's frequent recapitulations reveal. Their joyous intimate love, physical as well as mental, leads one to understand their conjugal bliss especially in the early years of their marriage. However, this happiness seems destined to drift as there is a basic incompatibility, a dissimilarity of temperaments. This novel is another example of the harshness in conjugal bliss. To begin with, Gopal informs Sumi about his parting from the villa. Next morning, he departs and leaves his wife and daughters to struggle alone. The fear of being unable to fulfill his obligations as a husband and as a father coupled with an intense loneliness and a feeling of seclusion from his wife and daughters, has compelled him to choose what could easily be termed a coward's way out. Sumi, the wife, feels extremely cloistered and hurt at the mental process of her fault-finding daughters. Their belief is against her. To them, Sumi is the reason of Gopal's action. According to N.B. Masal, "this novel is actually the exploration of a woman's inner life. Here the inner life of Sumi who is emotionally secluded from her family is reflected and refracted."[16] Gopal's absence from the family scene creates unique tension for various characters. In Sumi's life there is loneliness because of her husband's abandonment. The wife tries to find out clues to his probable motives in his past acts and utterances. Sumi knows that Gopal believes that "marriage is not for everyone. The demand it makes a lifetime of commitment is not possible for all of us."[17] The novel is more deeply involved in the relationship of husband and wife than any of Shashi Deshpande's other novels. It places the failed marriage of Sumi and Gopal at the centre, a marriage that does not have any of the accusations of the other and blame throwing matches and goes on to frame it with descriptions of other marriages. Sumi remembers that when they had decided to get married, Gopal proposed that if either of the two wanted to be free, he or she would be left to go. There should not be handcuffs to tie them together. The wife is, however, not unconscious of the developments taking place in him. As far as Gopal is concerned, his inward thoughts always remain unsaid to anybody. He is not able to explain even to his wife Sumi, the reason that compelled him so much as to seclude himself from his own family members. He only assures them that Sumi is in no way responsible for that decision and therefore she need not to be blamed. Though deserted by her husband for no fault of hers, Sumi learns to fight her own battle and assert her individuality. For Sumi, Gopal's desertion makes her experience the trauma of a deserted wife and the anguish of a secluded partner. She is seen gradually emancipating herself as a new and independent woman.

The hollowness of man-woman relationship is graphically illustrated in the saga of the marriage of Sumi's parents also in *A Matter of Time,* Kalyani and Shripati. Kalyani was an intelligent girl and was often playfully told by her father that she would become the country's first engineer. She was, however, not allowed to even complete her schooling, and instead was married off to her maternal uncle, Shripati, according to her mother's wishes. Kalyani's mother, Manorama, is obsessed with the fear of her husband taking up another wife as she could not produce a male heir to their property and she does not even relish the idea of Kalyani marrying into a new family, as the property would then belong to them. It was because after this Manorama felt secure. The property now would remain in the family itself. Hence her desire that her only child, Kalyani, should marry her brother, Shripati. Kalyani and Shripati have three children. The last one, who is a boy, is mentally retarded. Tragedy strikes Kalyani when her four-year-old son gets lost at railway station as she is waiting to board the train to Bangalore. Shripati do not forgive his wife for her negligence and sends her back to her parent's house with her two remaining children, Sumi and Premi. It is only on her death bed that Manorama is able to prevail upon her brother to return and live in the house with his wife and daughters. He obliges her but continues to maintain a stony silence with his wife. The husband and wife live like strangers under the same roof and have not spoken for years. It is a desertion in every way except that they live in the same house. The enormous cruelty of it, apparently, does not cause as much concern as it would have, if, Shripati had forsaken his wife, or she had died. But Kalyani, like a majority of women, accepts life as it is, and when she has to put her signature, she signs her name carefully as Kalyani Bai Pandit.

## 3.3 Marriage Provides Security to Woman

In some other cases marriages also provide security to woman. Mini in *Roots and Shadows*, is an important character in the novel whose marriage has been arranged by her parents. Although she is not actually married off in the novel. There are several indications as to the kind of man she is about to marry. The groom is neither highly educated nor good looking. He is much older than her. However, marriage with him does offer the prospect of security and a certain social status to Mini. But most women marry because they are expected to do so. Society expects them to get married. They also marry for economic security. When Mini has the option of choosing between Naren, a sensitive young man but not good in social terms, and an elder widower, Mini and her mother reject Naren. Mini's mother measures the bridegroom's worth in terms of the property that he owns. Mini is looked upon as a burden and a responsibility by her parents who are anxious to get her married off. Mini, on her part, is sensible and pragmatic and aware of the fact that a girl like her who is overage has a flawed horoscope and little dowry, cannot have better prospects and so she readily agrees to the match. Another reason is that she is brought up in a traditional way; marriage is the fulfillment of her destiny and her life's ambition. She is content with the practical side of marriage, happy in the knowledge that marriage would give her an enhanced status in society. For Mini, it was marriage that mattered, not the man. She is confident that once "she is married, and he becomes her husband none of his faults will matter." (RS, 139)

Similarly, in *That Long Silence,* Jaya's aunt Vanitamami represents one such passive acceptor. She is childless, unattractive, awkward, incompetent, and neglected by her husband. Yet, despite all odds, Vanitamami manages to love cheerfully. In true Hindu tradition, she accepts that husband is the wife's protector and believes that as long as one is a wife, one is secure. Her total faith in tradition makes it impossible for her to even think that she is oppressed.

Shashi Deshpande also gives us a glimpse of women living at another level of society, women like Shakutai and Sulu in *The Binding Vine*. Shakutai's husband leaves her in her father's home soon after their marriage so that he can search for livelihood in Bombay. When he does not return six months later, however, Shakutai joins him in Bombay, unable to stay any longer in her father's house. She realises that her husband is a lazy and good for nothing fellow who does not stick on to any job. They live in a relative's house where she is put through much humiliation. After the birth of three children one after the other, Shakutai takes it upon herself to work and support her family. Her husband deserts her for another woman. Shakutai does not hesitate to describe her husband as a useless fellow. It is, indeed, tragic that despite putting up with such a worthless husband and despite struggling alone to find a place for her children, fingers are pointed at her when anything goes wrong in the family as is the case when Kalpana is raped.

The married life of these women, whether working or non-working, ends in discontentment. The condition of Shakutai's sister Sulu is no better either. From all accounts, she comes across as a very affectionate and sweet natured person. She helps her sister in every way she can and tries to take over the responsibility of bringing up Kalpana which is, however, thwarted by Kalpana herself. As we learn later, she is lusted after by Prabhakar, Sulu's husband. Sulu was a very cheerful girl before marriage but after marriage she is changed. She always had a fear that her husband can throw her out at any time because she is childless.

The level of submission practiced by women in the interest of safeguarding their marriage is also hinted as a glimpse is offered into the marriage of Vanna and Harish. Vanna, an educated, cheerful and optimistic social worker, is submissive and willing to go along with her husband in whatever way he wants. She is solicitous and caring and does not resent her household duties. She, infact, is a woman who is a symbol of love and is a superwoman. She herself is a doctor and married to a doctor who makes a fetish of order and regularity. Vanna is conditioned to cater to his rigid timetables like a puppet and she gets very annoyed if Urmi teases her about it. Urmi is the more assertive of the two friends and often reprimands Vanna, whose constant refrain 'Harish says', irritates her terribly. Urmi is also angry with her when she later tells wistfully of her secret longing to have a son which is ruthlessly denied to her by her husband. After the birth of their second child who is also a daughter, Vanna tells Harish about her desire to have a son. But he quotes population figures to her and expresses surprise that she should be one of those women who crave for sons. And then, he also asks her why she should think for sure that the next child would be a son. Despite all these arguments, Vanna still feels that she would not have minded taking a chance.

The degree to which Indian women are subjected to domination by their husbands is also evident from what in *The Binding Vine,* Inni reveals to Urmi in reply to her unvoiced accusation against her parents for having left her to be brought up by her grandparents at Ranidurg. Inni pathetically confesses to Urmi that it was her father and Inni's husband who had sent her away. The reason is that he did not trust his wife with looking after the child well as she had left the child in the lurch. Years later when she tries to explain to Urmi the reason why she was sent away. Inni pours out all the anguish of a woman who was helpless before the dictates of her husband.

Evangeline Shanti Roy says that "a number of variations on the theme of man-woman relationships come up on the periphery of the plot-structure."[18] There is Vanna's mother Akka in the same novel, who was married by her father just to look after Mira's motherless baby, although she knew about her husband's obsession for his first wife. The marriage of Akka also proves how terribly unfair our society is towards women. She is made to marry a widower and the father of a child. Even before her marriage, she is warned that her prospective husband had been obsessed with his wife and after her death is now interested only in his son. Infact, he marries only so that his son can have a mother. This example, in a way, describes the fate of many women who socially accept marriage under any condition because marriage is the only goal in life for a girl in our society, and finding a groom is the most difficult thing on earth. So, Akka willingly agrees to marry Kishore's father despite the risk of living under the shadow of a dead woman.

## 3.4 Struggles between Body and Mind

Shashi Deshpande shows how the institution of marriage can sometimes shatter the self-confidence of a person and transform a vivacious girl into a fearful and nervous woman. Marriages in male oriented societies turn out to be dissatisfying for the female partner – both physically and spiritually. It creates confusion in her, whether to take up the path of submission or rejection because both end in discontentment. If viewed critically marriage is found to be degenerating where there is no involvement except in physical relationship and everything goes on mechanically to carry on life. As a result marriage becomes meaningless and sex alone seems to sustain the man-woman relationship.

Mira's story, seen from a woman's point, depicts Kishore's father as an uncaring man. Mira was Urmi's dead mother-in-law. She had been married at eighteen. Her story was revealed through the brief entries in her diary. These entries provide a glimpse into a life lived painfully and secretively. A chance encounter of Urmi with an old trunk in the attic of the house exposes her to the poems written by Mira. These poems bring alive to her the woman who wrote them in the solitude of an unhappy marriage and who died giving birth to her only son at the age of twenty-two. Through Mira's letters and poems, Urmi discovered a secluded woman who questioned silently the relevance of her traditional role of wife and mother. Mira was unhappy wife and she died while giving birth to her son, Kishore, with her development frozen at that stage. Prior to that, she has passed through hope and despair, self-hatred, and hatred of the other and the physical experience of motherhood. All these things capture in her responses, the hesitation and uncertainty of a young girl's life. In Mira's diaries, Urmi hears the cry against rape and the anguish of a talent that was crushed before it could flower. None of Mira's poems are about love as if she did not believe in it. They reveal her miserable life, cloistered in a home, living with a man she did not love, surrounded by people she had nothing in common with. Perhaps it was her writings that kept her alive. Akka tells Urmi how her father-in-law had been attracted to Mira, a college student, and how he had pursued and married her. Perusing the voluminous pile of writing left behind by the young Mira, Urmi fathoms the extent of forced physical relationship Mira was subjected to by her husband. Mira's innermost feelings find expression in her poems written in the vernacular, Kannada. Later, Urmi published them in English. A husband imposing himself on his wife is, however, never publicised at least among the Indians where the Puranas dictate that it is a wife's duty to please her husband in bed. Mira, perhaps, symbolises the plight of countless women who face the same situation but are unable to give voice to their suffering. The invasion of one's body, even though sanctified by marriage, can be as traumatic as rape. Later, through Mira's diaries Urmi discovers, her innermost feelings when she says, "Love: How I hate the word. If this is love, It is terrible thing." (BV, 67)

Shashi Deshpande, through Mira's story, presents the psychological violence of oppression within personal relationships. At the time when Urmi discovers Mira's poems and diaries, she also comes in contact with Kalpana. Kalpana, a young woman hanging between life and death in a hospital ward, is the victim of rape. In Mira's diaries also she hears the cry against rape. Kalpana's and Mira's life appear to bear similarities. Mira had been reduced to a stereotyped feminine role model, while Kalpana was yet another aspect of the submissive and passive portrayal of womanhood. In a largely hostile patriarchal culture, one of the ways in which women were dominated was either through a forced marriage, or through physical relationship by perverted acts like rape outside marriage. Kalpana, a teenaged girl from a tenement, is the victim of a gruesome rape and lies unconscious for more than four months, without any chance of recovery. At first sight there is nothing in common between Mira, married to man who is besotted with her, and this girl, cruelly raped and battered by an unknown assailant. It is only at the end of the novel that we realise how accurate Urmi's intuition is. Mira is raped by her own husband, while Kalpana's assailant is none other than her aunt Sulu's husband Prabhakar. Shakutai, the mother of Kalpana, who had been deserted by her husband, looked to Prabhakar who was "not a drunkard, or a wife beater or a waster," (BV, 193) to provide the father role-model to her children. Even when Prabhakar sent word to her through Sulu that he wanted Kalpana as his second wife, since Sulu was childless, and had also developed some skin disease, Shakutai agrees. She is furious with Kalpana for refusing the offer. It is when Prabhakar learns that Kalpana had fallen in love with another boy and wanted to marry him, he rapes her in frustration. Infact, there is little to choose between Mira's husband's lust and Prabhakar's, feels Urmi. Both of them had satisfied their lust without taking into consideration the feeling of the object of their desire. Neither Mira nor Kalpana could accept the men who were obsessed with them and lusted after their body, and yet could not escape. Mira died, giving birth to the baby born of her husband's lust, while Kalpana lies in a perpetual coma, a living death. Shashi Deshpande, in almost all her examinations of the man-woman relationship, stresses the fact that the legally, socially, and morally sanctioned physical relationship within marriage can deteriorate into the ugliest form of cruelty unless it grows out of mutual love, respect and understanding. The events in Akka's life in *Roots and Shadows,* serve to focus upon several issues related to the treatment and position of women in Indian society. One such issue is the practice of child marriage and its impact on the child-bride. Akka's traumatic girlhood is an example of the tragic consequences a young girl of thirteen could have had when she was married off to a fully grown, uncaring man double her age. At a tender age, she was subjected to such brutality that she began to regard physical relationship as punishment. She had tried to escape from her husband's house, but her mother-in-law had caught her and returned her to him. The mother-in-law locked her up and starved her for three days and then sent her back to her husband but there was no escape from him. Even before she is out of her teens, Akka becomes pregnant. Her immature, undeveloped body cannot give birth to a living child. This adds to her misfortunes, as she is branded inauspicious and evil because of her childlessness. Her childlessness, therefore, results in increased ill-treatment at her mother-in-law's hands. When her husband takes a mistress, she has some respite from his sexual demands. However, the incident reveals both the injustice to the young wife and the dual standards of morality, particularly as society allows a dissatisfied man to have an extra-marital affair. It also highlights the deeply ingrained belief that a woman exists only for the purpose of satisfying a man's needs.

## 3.5 The Dominance of Indian Morality

There are several women characters that are compelled to move from the romantic idea of love and marriage to a more realistic view of their relationships. They realise an immeasurable distance between the idea and the reality. The two people who get married do not lose or dissolve their identities, they remain two individual human beings and thus loneliness, disappointment and disagreement do fall to their lot. There is a whole world of understanding, of living together and of tenderness, which goes into its making. It is not enough also, in another way, for there is a life beyond it, a life of emotions, intellectual communication and understanding, and a life not necessarily based on physical relations. Marriage does not fulfill all the needs of woman, nor it provides emotional support to them, but they have someone to give support. Shashi Deshpande, delineate in her novels few male characters that give support to women who are deeply secluded. It is a kind of friendship that exists outside marriage whether between Saru and Boozie in *The Dark Holds No Terror,* Jaya and Kamat in *That Long Silence,* Indu and Naren in *Roots and Shadows,* and Urmi and Bhaskar in *The Binding Vine,* and Manjari and Raja in *Moving On.*

In *The Dark Holds No Terror,* Boozie so called by his students because his initial is B.O.Z, is Sarita's professor at the medical college. He has a definite air about him. Sarita is drawn towards him because he is audacious and rich unlike her husband, Manu. When Boozie displays interest in her, she is attracted to him as he has all that she has aspired for in a man like money, position, fame, power, romance. As their association grows, she deceives herself into believing that theirs is only a teacher-student relationship. It is not clear whether Sarita is attracted towards Boozie only because of his success or also for emotional reasons. Surprisingly, Sarita expects Manu to object to Boozie's flirtatious behaviour and when he does not do that, she begins to resent it: "I hated...... Manu for doing nothing." (DHNT, 94) Both in allowing Boozie to shape her and in wanting Manu to reprimand her, Sarita unconsciously exhibits the traditional need of women to be controlled and protected by a male. There are both the things in her behaviour – cunningness and immaturity. It is the cunningness that wants to enjoy her power over both men one for desiring her and the other for his weakness. Shashi Deshpande portrays the character of Boozie entirely through Sarita's eyes. She makes no attempt to individualise the character. One is not aware, for instance, of his motives in grooming Sarita or encouraging her in the climb to success.

Another important character is Naren in *Roots and Shadows*. He is an unconventional male character. Like Indu, he is motherless and has been brought up in the joint family in an old house. Indu, during her stay in the old house, discovers him to be a sensitive person who understands her problems and doubts, quite unlike Jayant, her husband. Naren is created as a foil to Jayant. While Jayant is fastidious and a perfectionist, Naren is careless and casual. Indu's relationship with Naren must be viewed in the light of her problems with Jayant. In Naren's company she can reveal her real self. Infact, her physical relationship with Naren helps her to realise what was wrong with her relationship with Jayant. Naren is a free person who has never bowed down to the dominant social mores and norms, while she, after marriage, has rapidly turned herself into the middle-class man's ideal wife. In the novel, Naren is a contrast to Jayant. He acts as a conscience-keeper for Indu; he reminds her of all the cherished values that she has suppressed. Unlike Jayant, he displays a genuine interest in her writing and is concerned about its deteriorating quality. This is more than solicitude and Indu is moved by it. In his criticism, she recognises Naren's genuine interest in her growth as a human being. It is Naren, who by his touch of love discovered Indu to herself, gave her the experience of release from shadow to existence and by her real self. Now through his attitude towards love helps her find one more piece of the jigsaw puzzle and that is her life with Jayant had become. Naren, through his acceptance of her rejection, makes her realise that what she wanted was involvement, not detachment.

Similarly, Kamat in *That Long Silence*, provides emotional support to Jaya. In the novel, Jaya hears again and again her neighbour Kamat's voice. Greying, middle-aged, bulky Kamat is Jaya's friend.

His open conversation and strong support for the short stories that she has written but suppressed slowly builds her confidence, bolstering her identity as a writer. He first makes Jaya aware of the connection between her passivity as a writer and as a woman. From him she learns firsthand that man and woman can be emotionally honest with one another. Recalling the dialogue, she cautiously finds new faith in the potential union between man and woman, giving her a measure of hope, and thus enriching her identity as a woman who wants to be paired with man. Kamat's relationship with her is that of a good friend. Jaya is pleasantly surprised and intrigued by the discovery. Kamat is deeply interested in Jaya's development as a human being and encourages her to express herself. Though he does not live long enough to know, he becomes one of Jaya's main catalysts for change. His words reverberate in her mind long after the fact, and she slowly understands she has used her story of herself as a suffering martyr to avoid taking action. But Jaya's companionship ended abruptly, however, when she acknowledged that he wanted to be her lover. She fled with a guilty conscience to avoid admitting that she also desires him as this desire clashes with her investment in the identity of single-minded, virtuous wife. Jaya realises that in order to attain self-hood, a woman must transcend silence, negation and seclusion. Mukta Atrey and Viney Kirpal delineate that "Shashi Deshpande's portrayal of Kamat presents him as the most liberated and prejudice-free of all the men characters in her novels."[19] He shows deep understanding of a woman's predicament and advocates that every woman must assert and develop herself to her full potential.

Naren in *Roots and Shadows* is also supportive of Indu; however, he is equally interested in her as a woman. Boozie in *The Dark Holds No Terrors* is the hero type person. Although his motives in encouraging her are not clear, he certainly aids her development by giving her financial support. This quality, to inspire the protagonists to grow and evolve, to express and assert them, is presented in all the three characters – Naren, Boozie and Kamat, the friends of the protagonists. By contrast, this quality is absent in their husbands. Dr. Bhaskar Jain and Urmila in *The Binding Vine,* are intellectual equals. Bhaskar does not contribute to her growth and development as the male friends of the other protagonists do. However, like Kamat and Naren, Bhaskar is good and dependable friend with whom a woman can freely share her innermost thoughts and emotions because she knows she won't be misunderstood or evaluated by the usual patriarchal norms of society. Dr. Bhaskar enables her to talk about the loss of Anu, about Ranidurg and about Baiajji. The understanding male friend with whom the protagonist can share everything but whom she does not marry, recurs in every novel of Shashi Deshpande. Bhaskar stands for the ideal companion that every woman seeks in a husband. Unlike Jaya who runs away from the dead Kamat to save her reputation, Urmila insists on continuing her friendship with Bhaskar openly. Taking a lift in his car occasionally, accepting a dinner date or going with him to his house to meet his mother, are simple expressions of a friendship between two professionals who enjoy each other's company. However, once again, Shashi Deshpande problematises the male friend and married woman relationship as Bhaskar grows serious in his intentions towards Urmila. Typically, he surmises that a woman whose husband is away for several months and who never speaks of him, could not be very happy in her marriage. Urmila feels cheated and angry – cheated because she had never thought of Bhaskar as a lover, and angry because she ought to have expected this development. Although Urmila chooses to remain faithful to Kishore, there is a momentary rebellion in her, as Indu-like, she wonders if she ought to have exorcised her disappointment in Kishore by giving to Bhaskar 'what he wants.'(BV, 165) The character of Bhaskar works largely to foreground her suppressed dissatisfaction with Kishore. It also enables her to recognise that she deeply loves her husband.

## Notes and References

1. Jasbir Jain. *Gendered Realities, Human Spaces: the Writing of Shashi Deshpande,* (Jaipur: Rawat Publication, 2003), 85.
2. S.P. Swain. "Shashi Deshpande's The Dark Holds No Terrors: Saru's Feminine Sensibility," *Indian Women Novelists*, Set I, Vol.4, ed. by R.K. Dhawan, (New Delhi: Prestige Books, 1990), 35-36.
3. Shashi Deshpande. *The Dark Holds No Terrors*, (New Delhi: Penguin Books, 1990), 37, here after cited in the chapter.
4. Shashi Deshpande. *Roots and Shadows*, (Hyderabad: Disha Books, 1992), 67, here after cited in the chapter.
5. Shashi Deshpande. *The Binding Vine*, New Delhi: Penguin Books, 1993, 137, here after cited in the chapter.
6. Shashi Deshpande. *Small Remedies*, (New Delhi: Viking, Penguin, 2000), 137, here after cited in the chapter.

7. Ranjini Jyoti Singh. "Quest For Space and Selfhood in Shashi Deshpande's Small Remedies", *Pegasus*, Vol.4, Jan-Dec 2005, 24.
8. Shashi Deshpande. *If I Die Today*, (New Delhi: Vikas Publishing House, 1982), 24, here after cited in the chapter.
9. Shashi Deshpande. *That Long Silence*, (London: Virgo Press, 1988), here after cited in the chapter.
10. Sarla Palkar. "Breaking The Silence, Shashi Deshpande's That Long Silence", *Indian Women Novelists*, Set I, Vol.V, 166.
11. Siddhartha Sharma. Shashi Deshpande's Novels: A Feminist Study, (New Delhi: Atlantic Publishers & Distributors, 2005), 38.
12. Y.S. Sunita Reddy. *A Feminist Perspective on The Novels of Shashi Deshpande*, (New Delhi: Prestige Books, 2001), 79.
13. Indira Bhatt. "That Long Silence: A Study," *Indian Women Novelists*, ed. by. R.K. Dhawan, (Delhi: Prestige Books, 1991), 42.
14. Adele King. "Effective Portrait," Debonair, June 1988, 97.
15. Veena Sheshadri. "That Long Silence", *Literature Alive*, II, I, 1988, 94.
16. N.B. Masal. "Shashi Deshpande's A Matter of Time: As an Exploration of a Woman's Inner Life", ed. by. T.M.J. *Indra Mohan, Shashi Deshpande: A Critical Spoctrum*, (New Delhi: Atlantic Publishers & Distributors, 2004), 144.
17. Shashi Deshpande. *A Matter of Time*, (New Delhi, Penguin books, 1996), 69. Here after cited in the chapter.
18. Evangeline Shanti Roy. "Shashi Deshpande's The Binding Vine: A Quest for the Anchor of Life", *Littcrit*, Vol.27, No.1-2, June-December 2001, 80.
19. Mukta Atrey, Viney Kirpal. "Shashi Deshpande's: A Feminist Study Of Her Fiction", (New Delhi: B.R. Publishing Corporation, 1998), 56.

## CHAPTER 4

# Motherhood

Motherhood is a dominant feature of Shashi Deshpande's novels. The bond between mother and a child is primordial. The main destination behind study about motherhood is to take the wraps off the crux of this crucial and closest affinity. The relationship between the mother and the child is very strong. They experience everything together and at times their experience converges but it could diverge also, leading to communication gaps. The novels of Shashi Deshpande lend a hand to expose the suffocation, panic, fear, frustration, care, love and helplessness associated with the scene of Indian motherhood.

Indian mother, traditionally, is a revered figure. She is always respected. Though mother principle is a mythological story, but it is all pervasive. Our rivers and our country are mother, and our very own planet earth is also mother for all of us. Even our goddesses of art, music, knowledge, and wealth are mothers – Lakshmi, Sharda, Saraswati. According to Usha Bande: "In fairy tales and legends it is the benevolent elderly woman who is always the personification of the mother."[1] Mother puts a very strong and secure hold on Indian people's psyche. The repository of all positive values which influence the quality of life and ultimately transform the society is mother. Thus, mother's role is of profound value to the well-being of society. She symbolises creativeness and continuity. In her absence, survival of people and society is almost impossible. Even man's spiritual existence is nullified without her. Transgressing her authority is, therefore, both a sin and a vice. Children, male and female, are supposed to subordinate and submit before her. She is given high respect and honour in society and myth, legend, religion, and tradition. Given the importance of mother in Indian culture, it is not surprising that it should be a major theme in twentieth century Indian English fiction. Much of the aura surrounding the mother in the Vedic, Puranic or the Brahamanic period, is missing though-flushed away by the massive movement of history. During the intervening period of foreign invasion and colonial rule, the ideological foundation laid by our forefathers still holds fast to an extent. Although the lived realities of life have now tempered the image of mother and it is no longer idealised beyond recognition, the mother, even today, is the cultural sanctifier, the redeeming force, the sustainer of life. In life and literature, the mother now no longer appears to be a mother Goddess, a glorified goddess of superhuman strength and weakness, her magnanimity and greed, her powerlessness, and her frustrations.

We might feel that woman's subjection as a wife to her husband is compensated by her dominant role as a mother over her son – a role that gives her true fulfillment. The dominance of woman as a creative principle or mother is reinforced by prehistoric findings. It is however, possible to take a fresh look at this emphasis on the assumption of male supremacy. Certain specific duties performed by male in family, defence of the community against external danger etc. leads to this supremacy. Motherhood is venerated but not fully understood. It is viewed as the completion of a process begun through male initiative and the mother is a figure which merges easily with the background. The conventional patterns of behaviour make mothers, taking care of family needs and managing household affairs, giving comfort to rest of the family at the cost of personal need, comfort, and privacy. Mother appears as an ideal and idol to boys. A typical male ideal construct is adoring her and placing her on a pedestal. Mother's single step away from traditional line can send a child hurtling down with a broken image. A child can develop confidence in self as well as in others by the fundamental benevolence of mother. A safe environment, away from hostile world, is provided by mothers. A girl child fails to internalise womanhood if a mother leaves her in lurch. Her sense of identity and self-get lost away. She is left all alone unaided in the hostile world with baffling physical and emotional changes which in turn gives rise to a confused life. She becomes unable to gear up to face life and its realities. Girl's only friend, who gives her identity sense and helps her to tide over the traumatic growing up period successfully, is mother. Display of many changes in the portrayal of mothers and mother figures is done by the fast-changing Indian society under modern western culture.

Shashi Deshpande displays a feminist bent in dealing with the mother. According to K.C. Baral, "The mother as a woman is on self-quest that expand from day-to-day struggle of existence to the higher realisation of the selfhood. In depicting mother-daughter relationship Shashi Deshpande makes it clear that the daughter is not ready to accept the image of the mother that would be again her own. The daughter struggles to be free from the stereotype role model and desires to exist as an individual and not as type."[2] In the novels, mother is displaced from the hallowed alter of worship to the mother among us. She is no more a deity but a woman of today, facing and challenging the realities of day-to-day life. The archetypal terrible mother and mother earth no longer seems to exist. Rather she is one among the erring humans which are liable to be charged, implaced and discarded in life and even after death. A step towards self-consciousness and a demand for feminist autonomy is in the novels of Shashi Deshpande. There is a beginning of a new beginning. The overall picture of mothers is divided into some categories. Some mothers are traditional and conventional. Some of them are literate and self-dependent mothers while others are passive mothers. Mothers in the novels of Shashi Deshpande are secluded figure, working within their limited preview with complete dominance by men and harassment by in-laws along with misunderstanding by daughters. Jasbir Jain has rightly said about motherhood that "Motherhood actually places a huge burden on a woman, for not only does she have to nurture the child, but her relationship with the child is a strong formative influence on the child, especially if the child is a daughter."[3]

This is more true of Indian families where children are especially supervised than in western nations where more freedom is granted to them. In doing so, there is always a restriction of space and privacy in case of joint families. In some or the other way the motherhood quality relates to the way of how these women perceive themselves. A more significant and important question to be put on, is to look at motherhood itself which is an offshoot of wifehood. Woman's relationship with husband may also alter that with the children. How does mother feel in case of being an unhappy wife and how does she feel when she is marginalised and excluded like Inni's mother? Mother daughter relationship cannot be named as a one-to-one relationship. The male presence, the husband or the son, shapes and governs the relationship. Mother seeks fulfillment by her children and looks for satisfaction as does kalpana's mother in her relationship with her sister. Shashi Deshpande, by focusing on these relationships brings out the complexity of social web, which work in innumerable way. In *Small Remedies*, Savitribai Indorekar, rejects Munni, her daughter and completely erases her away from her articulated memories, thereby projecting another consequence of motherhood. In *The Binding Vine,* Urmi is not able to understand Inni's submissiveness in her marriage and her seeming indifference to motherhood. Similarly, Saru works herself into a position where her hidden fears are exorcised. Urmi, Saru and Jaya are mothers themselves, thus they are better able to relate their own mothers once they have overcome the sense of insecurity. At some level, the discovery of motherhood by woman herself is a search of the way it subtracts from personhood. Madhu in *Small Remedies*, grieving the loss of her son, Aditya, is analysing her possessive obsession with the child and how letting him go was problematic for her. Leaving him at home for an evening was an agony. The inability to do so is to see the child, as an extension of the mother's being. It is an inability to recognise the child's Individuality or independent identity, no matter whether it is a son or a daughter. According to Jasbir Jain, "Motherhood is egocentric; it gives a sense of power, power that women may not necessarily wield in the wider social world. The wish to control the child is camouflaged as concern and manifested as caring, but it is also a fulfillment for the ego. It is here where a woman feels indispensable." (J.J, 60) The alteration in the concept of motherhood does not entirely lie in the matter of individual personality, insecurity, of the kind of relationship with the husband, or culturally governed through socialisation and myths but it also responds to social change and space for woman in other roles. They go outside of limited confining categories of oppression, aggression, and growth in stature. The main focus of this chapter motherhood lies in the fluidity existing among them and centering of mother as a subject.

## 4.1 Traditional mothers

In *The Dark Holds No Terrors*, the mother of Saru is a domineering lady, who tries to control others without being aware of their views and feelings. In other words, she is an orthodox, traditional, old fashioned and an altogether different person. A person moulded by tradition, constraint and anger. She brought her children up with some amount of strict discipline. As Sarbjit Sandhu aptly remarks: "The mother is very attached to her son. Her attitude is a typical one – after all, he is male child and therefore one who will propagate the family lineage. In another sense, also, the male child is considered more important than a girl, because he is qualified to give "agni" to his parents. The soul of the dead person would otherwise wander in forment."[4] On the other hand, the mother is stricter with her daughter Saru. She is of the view that a daughter is always a responsibility. She has to get married and has to go in her husband's home. And for this, a daughter should be trained to submit and adjust in a new household. For sons, it is totally different. No household chores for them, these were meant for daughters only. The son has to earn bread for the whole family. He is the one who would carry on the family name and light the pyres of his parents. It is totally a conventional and orthodox mode of thinking. By thinking in this manner, the mother neglects her daughter. Ragini Ramachandra however feels that this aspect of the story does not ring true. She writes: "The portrayal of Sarita's mother who adored the son and neglected the daughter seems to be a weak point in the story. While one could accept a mother's preferences amongst her children, it seems rather incredible that she should live and die with curses on her lips for her female child, especially in the Indian context. The mother's monstrosity seems to serve as a rallying point for the novelist to bring her feminist ideas together. Hence the nagging feeling that the book has an axe to grind."[5] Mother is suffering from gender discrimination and with this gender bias, there aroused a huge space between the mother and the daughter. The lack of communication leads them towards seclusion. Saru starts hating her mother. There are numerous occasions when the mother shows her concern for the daughter, but the attitude is always conventional and traditional which the daughter takes in other way. The mother shows gender difference in her treatment of her son Dhruv and the daughter as we find recorded in Saru's conversation with the mother, "Don't go out in the sun you'll get even darker." Who cares?" "We have to care if you don't. We have to get you married." "I don't want to get married." Will you live with us all your life?" Why not?" You can't." And Dhruv?" "He's different. He's a boy."[6] These lines show the mother's preference for her son as well as the concern for her daughter, but the way of expression is traditional. The preference for boys is blatantly acknowledged in most Indian families. In other way, the mother wants to teach her daughter the traditional social way of living from which she herself had to pass but in doing this she becomes harsher towards her. Saru's mother's attitude is typical of most Indian mothers, but it creates an opposite effect on Saru's psyche. As Rashmi Sahi observes: "Mother and daughter share a gender identity, a social role and social expectations. In mothering a baby girl, a woman is bringing her daughter to be like her, to be a girl and then a woman. Because of the social consequences of gender, the mother inevitably relates differently to their sons and daughters."[7] The mother is a dominant figure in the novel who herself decides what is for son and what is for daughter. In doing this on one occasion Saru became more important than Dhruv. There was an occasion when the daughter of the house could apply attar with tiny altar drenched swaks of cotton to the backs of women's hand. Sprinkle rose water over them and distributes the flowers but at the same time Dhruv started crying and the mother scolds him not the daughter. Mother said that "it's not for you. That's for girls." (DHNT, 57)

The mother is totally traditional who cares for both her children, but she is not able to guide her daughter in traditional manner. According to Mrinalini Sebestian: "Mother is an unloving, uncaring woman, who is only concerned about her dead son. Yet there are subtle indications of love as well as of the unequal relationship this mother shared with the father"[8], as the following passage makes it clear: "I went home and told her nothing but that I had obtained a first class. 'Good', she said. No more. But that night there was something special for dinner, something fried, something sweet, and I knew she was pleased, though her face told me nothing." (DHNT, 141) She is unable to come out of the traditional environment. Rather she takes pride in that. She disagrees and feels less enthusiastic about her daughter's education. It is true that in this novel, after Dhruv's death, the figure of mother became more than of the mother in-law. She blames her daughter for the death of her son. It is the strange behaviour of Saru that increased the sense of frustration and hatred in her mother. The mother herself is deeply secluded after her son's death; moreover, the behaviour of Saru has transformed her into a worse mother. It is true the motherhood is definitely affected by the behaviour of children. Why do children expect too much from mother? Mother also needs the love and care of the children. There is a problem of non-communication. Saru never tries to understand the inner feelings of her mother. When the mother needs consolation from her, she leaves the house and after some time married to a man of her own choice. Here one can find the importance of children in the life of mother. Children are the companions of future. They are the fillers of house and the lives of its inhabitants. All these things lead the mother towards frustration, "Is that all? A painted tray. An empty house. One child dead. Another alienated. And then the final reward …… pain, suffering and death." [DHNT, 108] These lines clearly show the reality of the family. There are several occasions when the parents cannot fulfill child's expectations or non-reliable desires. As a consequence, the child gets rebellious. The same thing happens with Saru. The mother gets extremely annoyed at the rebellious act of Saru and in her utmost frustration, she declares: "Daughter? I don't have any daughter. I had a son and he died. "Now I am childless …." [DHNT, 109] The mother erased all the memories of her daughter from her household with the exception of a photograph, only because her brother was also in it. In her seclusion and frustration, she refuses to see the doctor even while dying of cancer reiterates the idea of total rejection.

It is not necessary that a mother feels seclusion because of hatred towards the daughter; seclusion can come in any state of loneliness. The mother figure Shakutai in *The Binding Vine,* is also a kind of traditional and conventional mother. Shakutai, a working and lower middle-class woman, belongs to a conservative background. In the novel she is the only important character that is not educated. Yet her agonies are reaching out for meaning in the utter darkness which surrounds her, puts her at the same level as the sensitive, educated characters. The mother in the novel is a frustrated one. Shakutai is the mother of three daughters and one son. The elder daughter Kalpana is brutally raped and badly wounded. According to Basavaraj Naikar: "Frustrated motherhood of a different kind is depicted in the novel through the picture of another woman, Shakutai."[9] At the beginning, when she learns that her daughter has been raped, she wants the fact to be suppressed because no one would marry her daughter. She does not want to reveal this fact to anyone. The mother feels helpless and frustrated. Although she is very well aware that Kalpana has also undergone severe head injury and is on the verge of death. The mother requests the doctor not to inform the police. She says to Urmi, "No, no, no. Tell him, tai, it's not true, don't tell anyone, I'll never be able to hold up my head again, who'll marry the girl, we're decent people."[10] Shakutai's helplessness and sorrows are unlimited. Uneducated, poor, and abandoned by her husband, she has to suffer from disgrace and dishonour. Siddhartha Sharma observes: "Most Indian mothers would react in a similar way as they are concerned about their daughter's marriage. The novelist has evocatively laid bare Shakuntala's agony, anger, helplessness, and fear."[11] She is worried about the marriage of Kalpana, who is, in the words of doctor, neither dead nor alive.' (BV, 86) But actually women like Kalpana's mother find security in marriage. Shakutai shows so much concern for daughter. There are instances when she feels proud of her. She expresses her surprise at having given birth to a pretty child like Kalpana. She is full of praise when she talks about her daughter's physical appearance: "She's very pretty. She's not like me at all. When she was born, she was so delicate and fair, just like a doll, I wondered, how a woman like me could have a daughter like that." (BV, 93) This shows Shakutai's love for her daughter. She loves her like anything. That is why on seeing her daughter in this pitiable condition, the mother feels helpless. In her frustration she started blaming her. Shakutai tries to give her daughters all the facilities which were denied to her like good education, a good job and a respectable marriage. But all her dreams are shattered by her daughter's reckless and brainless behavior like painting her lips, dressing herself up and moving about with strangers, without knowing her own limitations. As a mother Shakutai was afraid of the boys of her chawl because they behave "like dogs panting after bitches." (BV, 146) Shakutai's complex emotions – her love for her daughter, her pride in her intellect and beauty, her irritation at her defiance of conventions, her fatalistic acceptance of woman's traditional role, are conveyed brilliantly through her.

The mother who keeps meandering between praising her daughter and criticising or blaming her, is a victim of her own values. Yet she was not born with these values embedded with in her mother's womb. Someone has to shape these values, make her believe that they were her own. The mother's reaction, no doubt, is a reflection of the society we live in, governed by age old patriarchy norms. Shakutai is also suffering from this. She feels deeply secluded on finding herself in that position where she has to bring up and married her other two daughters. On seeing Kalpana's pitiable condition she feels secluded in her life and in her utmost frustration she declares, "My children have become a burden to me, Urmila, they have become a burden." (BV, 147) There is another example of her frustration when she says to Urmi, "Why does God give us daughters." (BV, 150) As a traditional mother, Shakutai does not want that people know about the incident of Kalpana because according to her it will destroy the lives of her other daughters. The mother's reaction is that of a typical Indian mother bred in an oppressive male dominated society. Mother like Shakutai must be incomprehensible, with fear of the daughters not getting married or with their fear that they would not be able to hold up their head again. Shashi Deshpande has also given the examples of the mothers of her contemporary age. They are educated and self-dependent women.

## 4.2 Mothers of the Contemporary Age

The mother figure Saru in *The Dark Holds No Terror,* is highly self-willed. She is an educated and career-oriented mother, and her problems ensure because of her outsized ego and innate love for power over others. She has always been a problem child and the mother a problem one; that feeling leaves Saru frightened of the possibility of repetition of the cycle in the family too. She is least mother like in her reluctance to be on the giving side and grows highly impatient even with the eating habits of the children. She is the mother of two children Renu, the daughter and Abhi her son. When she looks towards her family she feels: "And as I looked, I could see them, my husband, and children, Abhi hidden by his father, Renu looking tiny by his side. Sitting there in that bright glass-enclosed room, watching them move away, I felt a deadly fear. As if I was isolated from everyone, from the whole world, by what was happening to me; that I was doomed to sit and watch happiness, watch it recede from me; doomed never to participate in it, never experience it myself." (DHNT, 112)

Saru's attitude towards children is invariably conditioned by her past and even love for importance. Saru is very indulging in her problems with her husband Mohan. And due to her psychological tensions, she neglects her children. She describes the eating habits of her children. She says Abhi loves butter; he gouges large bits out of the pack with a spoon. The mother does not like it but all the time his father defends him, and it enrages her more. On the other hand, there is Renu who delicately does it. But the mother is also not satisfied with it. As a mother, Saru is very sensitive. She wants that her children give some importance to her, but she is rather neglected by her children most of the time. She tries to give all the comforts, love, and affection to her children which she could not gain from her own. But even then, the children disappoint her. She often thinks, "Was she an unnatural, unloving mother? She had sworn that she would never fail her children in love and understanding as her own mother had done." (DHNT, 161)

The mother in her occasionally, comes to the fore front and feels guilty of having denied her children the love of grandparents. Though it is not in tune with the character of Saru, it is the thought of children that prevents her from seeking a divorce and she is cautious not to let them know of her problem with Manu. She loves her children very much. When she goes away to her father's house, she does remember the little needs of the children, like seeing Renu off to school every morning and covering Abhi with a blanket every night. But such a thought does not send her rushing home. Saru is explaining that Renu's verbal non-communication and eloquent, mystifying expressions in drawing leave Saru nervous: "What is this, Renu? A forest. A thick forest. And this child .... Why is she laughing? Because she feels like it you see..." (DHNT, 33) Here the lines show the depth of her psyche. A thick forest is a symbol of her loneliness. For a child the world is like a forest. What is in the forest? All lost, nothing is clear, uncarved for, totally darkness, lack of light. In this darkness mother has to show the right way to the child and if the child remains silent, then develops a kind of seclusion in both the lives. Saru refers to Renu as "a woman despite her age, a critical, cold, shrewd, objective observer," (DHNT, 49) reminiscent of her own mother. It speaks for Saru's projection and the unconscious fear of getting rejected by the daughter. She also entertains fear of the repetition of the cycle in her family as she finds in Renu's jealousy and rejection of Abhi a parallel of her attitude to Dhruv. She says: "Do we travel not in straight lines, but in circles? Do we come to the same point again and again? Dhruv and I, Renu and Abhi......is life an endless repetition of the same pattern?" (DHNT, 158)

Saru is actually very sensitive regarding her relationship with her daughter. It may be one of the reasons of making much of the children's birthdays with parties and games because she does not want to behave like her own mother. She has never had the kind of relationship daughters ordinarily have with their mothers. And she has passed on some of the same hostility to her own relationship with her daughter. Saru says about her daughter: "She reminds me of a room whose doors are closed. Nothing emerges, neither her joys nor her sorrows." (DHNT, 49)

It clearly shows that there is a lack of communication in parent child relationship that makes the relationship unbearable and leads to seclusion and isolation in the life of the characters. According to Gowri Sivaraman: "Jaya has her own past which intervenes with her present-day existence which is also beset with too many problems."[12] Jaya in *That Long Silence,* is sensitive, observant, questioning, determinedly objective mother. She is the mother of two teenage children Rahul and Rati, aborts her third pregnancy and feels guilty and remorse. Her guilt weakens her image of modern woman. The inability to communicate honestly with her children had always troubled her. Silence was there in Jaya's life.

As a mother Jaya realises her failure. Her seclusion is further accentuated as she ponders over the intrinsic loneliness of the human condition. To add to her despair, she gets the news that her son Rahul, who had been holidaying with their family friends, suddenly disappeared. This piece of news shatters her and hits her with the force of a bolt striking a tender tree. Later Rahul returns and she receives a telegram from Mohan that all is well. Before this happens, however, she lives for several days in a traumatic state: "A mother? Despairingly I relinquished my halo. No, I had been unfitted to be trusted with the entire responsibility of another human being. How had I dared to take it on? Mohan's wife, Rahul's, and Rati's mother. I can crawl into that hole, I had thought, a warm and safe hole; but here I was now prodded out of it by cruel, sharp staves."[13] The children become hostile towards their parents because parents are always involved in their own strives. This sort of hostility increases Jaya's dilemmas with consequent seclusion. Like her husband Mohan, she too puts her children into the slots and feels disappointed when they refuse to remain there and contribute their share in creating the myth of a happy and harmonious family. It is only at the end, after her ordeal, that Jaya realises her mistake and releases herself as well as her children from the slots into which she had put them.

Another mother figure Urmila is an educated and self-dependent woman who is a college teacher. She is the mother of two children. In this novel Urmi is coping with her own tragedy. She has lost a daughter and a son left. In this novel, she is grieving over the death of her one-year-old baby daughter Anu and in this condition she becomes highly sensitive. Urmi is very attached to her daughter, and it is her intense attachment that becomes the cause of her suffering. She grieves behind the closed door of the room that also shows seclusion in her life. It is pain at the loss of a child and the loss of the future within her, the future that will never open out now. She nourishes the pain within her for it allows her to be with the child. There is no way she can move out of this anguish. This pain leads her towards seclusion. Urmi says," This pain is all that's left to me of Anu. Without it, there will be nothing left to me of her; I will lose her entirely." (BV, 9) Urmi remembers the moment of Anu's death when her heart had stopped beating. But the pain has frozen her. Her depression pushes her into asthmatic attacks and leaves her with a physical sense of emptiness, an anguish that she cannot give to anyone for safekeeping. She finds it difficult to let go her memories. For Urmi the loss is terrible and despite the efforts of her friends and family members she clings on to grief. Commenting on her attitude, S. Indira writes: "Instead her pain and sorrows, she holds on to it as she believes that to let go of that pain, to let it become a thing of the past would be a betrayal and would make her lose Anu completely. Like a masochist, she clings to her pain and allows her memories of Anu, every small incident to flood her with longing and a great sense of loss."[14] Although she tries to fight the loss, she feels that forgetting this loss would tantamount to betrayal. But she has a son kartik and she has to live for him. As she reassures Kartik that she will not die, she realises that her will to live is still there, "No, I must reject these memories, I have to conquer them. This is one battle I have to win if I am to go on living." (BV, 21)

As a mother she realises her responsibility that Kartik needs her love but in her depression, she neglects her. It is the loss of relationship with a daughter that makes her ignored of her son. Mother's rich emotional texture of the piece is overpowering as it fluctuates between statement and silence and moves to and fro between anguish, helplessness, and expectation. Urmi never forgets to praise her son Kartik who is very quiet and decent. She says, "Even as a baby he was no quiet, it sometimes frightened me – could a normal human being be so placid? Now I know he is perfectly normal, but I worry about the way he can hold things with in himself."(BV, 76) Urmila often thinks that woman always takes parenthood seriously, but man does not take it seriously. Urmi as a mother is very sensitive and touched towards her children and it is motherhood that makes her blind, it almost brainwashes her. A mother can never be harsh with her own child. Urmila may neglect her son but she loves him too. When Inni, Urmila's mother, places the photograph of Anu on the wall, she refused it. She rejects the idea of having a framed photograph of Anu on wall. According to her, Anu lies in her heart, and she can remember each and every moment of her life. She is the part of her life and to recall her, there is no need to look at her picture, the only need is to look at Urmi's inner self: "I don't need to put up Anu's picture on the wall. I don't need a picture to remember her; I can remember every bit of her, every moment of her life. How can you imagine I need a picture…?" [(BV, 68)] It clearly shows the importance of children in mother's life. The death of her baby daughter sweeps away all the happiness in her life and brings seclusion in her life. There is one instance when her friend Lalita asked her about her children and she declared that, "Only one, a son…..the words keep hammering in my mind. How could I, oh God, how could I? That was betrayal, treachery, how could I deny my Anu?" [(BV, 106)] This is the thing Urmi cannot ignore in her life. This is a kind of loss, a loneliness and seclusion that cannot be filled. The seclusion is deep rooted in her soul.

Madhu in *Small Remedies* is secluded both physically and emotionally from her son Aditya. Adit is killed in a bus that is burnt down in Bombay, during the riots following the demolition of the Babri Masjid. That is the most tragic event in the life of the mother. The sudden death of her son Adit overwhelms her with a sorrow that affects her whole being. Thoughts pass unchecked through her mind. The mother is deeply touched by the death of her only son. When Adit does not return for three days after leaving home, her husband is called to identify him. This is touchingly recalled through the thoughts of the mother. It will take few days after the son's death that the mother reconciles herself with great difficulty, to the fact of his death. Som, her husband says to Madhu, "He's dead, Madhu, our son is dead. Listen to me, just listen, he's dead. I cremated him myself. Adit is dead, Madhu, he's gone, stop waiting for him."[15] Madhu is actually a bereaved mother. She enclosed herself in a fog of bereavement. Ranjini Jyothi Singh observes: "This is the most tragic event narrated in the novel. The sudden death of her son Adit overwhelms her with a sorrow that affects her whole being. Thoughts pass unchecked through her mind."[16] She is a deeply wounded person, riddled with her own demons, in deep grief over the death of her son and thrown into an irresolvable quandary over the estrangement from her husband. She is essentially, a secluded individual, quietly and steadfastly working in puzzle out the life of the elderly Savitribai so that she can write her biography both as a worthy project in itself and as a form of distraction to take her mind off her own dilemmas. All the time she recalls each and every memory of Adit. She was very happy with her son. Though motherless as a child, she on her part is a very caring mother conscious of every little need of her son, Aditya: "The baby is so small, so frail, so vulnerable how can I, how will I keep it safe? The little opening in the skull terrifies me. And the wispy neck that threatens to snap at a touch. How could Nature be so stupid as to allow these things? I'm in a cold sweat each time someone picks up the baby, I can't bear to see my mother-in-law do it, she holds him so casually, surely she'll drop him, his head is drooping backwards, can't she see that…" (SR, 89) The mother is so sensitive. She has only one thing to do and that is take care for Adit. He is everything for her. She does not have the time for someone else. She was very happy with him. When she saw Adit's face for the first time, she forgot all her tensions, her sufferings, and her problems. From that day Adit is her world. She declares: "Adit, Adit …. all my happiness, all my moments of joy centre round him. As he grouse, my world enlarges." (SR, 150)

The mother is totally shattered when she listens the dreadful news of her son's death. Madhu blames Som for the death of her son. Unfortunately for both of them, it is on one of those days when they are quarreling that Adit comes and finds them struggling together. While Madhu and Som are tormenting each other with the past and quarreling, Adit enters the scene. The seventeen-year-old boy wants to know why his parents are abusing with each other. It has the opposite effect on the mind of the child. They asked him to go away, and he died. He was very disturbed. The mother constantly thinks about this incident. This leads her towards seclusion. She says, "Motherhood absorbs all of me, I've nothing left for anyone, for anything" (SR, 146)

Another mother figure Manjari (Jiji) in *Moving On*, is an educated and sensitive mother. She has two children Anand and Sachi. She lives secluded in a house. The children want to live separately according to their own wish. There is seclusion and a blank space in the life of the mother. She often feels that "Anand and Sachi went away and left alone in the house, I found myself inhabiting what I could only think of as a blank space."[17] Jiji's Baba has given her the house which the children want to sell. They insisted on their mother for selling the house. Why do the children never care about the feelings of their mother? Why do they never think about their mother? They never care in what condition or what difficulties she has to face in living alone in that house. The mother's thinking about her own children can very well be guessed in her words: "I must be one of the few unfortunate mothers whose children have higher standards than her them." [(MO, 68)] As a mother, she is always indulging in her grief. The mother has sent her children away from her so that they do not dare to ask about their father and about the past life of her. But her daughter Sachi is more cautious of the behaviour of the mother. The mother has to behave according to the wish of the daughter. The daughter does not like that her mother speaks to any stranger. At times her behaviour is intolerable. Sachi is not interested in her mother's life, but she is always curious about her activities. By the behaviour of her children, the mother feels deeply frustrated. In her own tensions, she neglects her children and tries to stay away from them. Involved in her own problems, she feels secluded. She even cannot share that with her children because they will never understand her. There is a kind of gap, a space between Jiji and her children that makes her an unsuccessful mother.

## 4.3 Passive Mothers

Another category of mothers in the novels of Shashi Deshpande is that of passive mothers. The mother figure Inni, in *The Binding Vine,* is a passive mother. She was totally dominated by her husband. The mother has to suffer because she cannot make her husband believe that she can also be a good mother. She had once left her daughter, Urmila alone with a man. It was to punish the wife for that single mistake that the husband had not permitted her to bring up the daughter after that. As a mother it was really frustration for her. The mother has to lead a secluded life. She loves her daughter very much but even then; she is not allowed to express her love in front of her own daughter. On the other hand, the daughter takes it negatively. She often feels that her mother always neglects her. There is non-communication which creates a lot of unhappiness and seclusion in the life of the mother. On seeing Urmi's grieving over her dead daughter, she started crying. She cannot control herself and reveals the reality to her: "I shouldn't have left you alone with your Aju after

Bai died,' he confessed another time. That was no situation for a child of fifteen to cope with." (BV, 113) It clearly shows her sense of remorse. As a mother Inni is also failure. She being a passive mother couldn't express her love for her own daughter. She is a highly sensitive and frustrated soul. The mother thinks that she is not worthy to be called a mother because she has not given the love and affectation to her own daughter. It shows that mother-child is not a one-to-one relationship. It is governed and shaped by the male presence, the husband, or the son, in its finer nuances. There is another mother figure in the novel *The Binding Vine,* Vanaa, is an educated woman and a doctor by profession. She is the mother of two daughters Mandira and Pallavi. The mother is frustrated by the behaviour of her daughter Mandira. The daughter does not want her mother to leave them in the care of maid servant. She often complains about her mother's work outside. The mother is a professional lady. She finds herself in a fuss. In the novel, the mother always blames herself for not co-operating with her daughter. There is a lack of understanding and need of self-expression. But Mandira does not want to understand anything. Vanaa is deeply frustrated with the words of her daughter when she calls her a terrible mother. The mother says to her childhood friend, "Do you think there's something wrong with me, Urmi? Am I such a terrible mother?" (BV, 74) We can find that there is seclusion in the life of the mother. On the other hand, the mother has a passionate wish for a son, but her husband is not agreeing with her. Most of the time the mother is haunting with this thought. Moreover, the behaviour of the child creates several problems for her. As a mother Vanaa, always worries about her daughter. She is deeply hurt by the behaviour of their own daughter Mandira when she feels jealous of her own sister. The daughter keeps demanding that the mother should not be working and should not leave her daughter alone in the house. In her utmost frustration she says, "Why are these kids so demanding, Urmi?" (BV, 74) The mother is unable to cope up with the grudge and rage of her daughter. All the time the mother remains in her own problems and tensions. It leads her towards seclusion. She needs an inner space for her where she can define or express herself. As a mother Vanaa also gets failure in her life.

In *A Matter of Time,* Kalyani, is the mother of three children – Sumi, Premi, and a son. She has lost her four year mentally retarded son. This happened at the railway station. The son wandered away as she was attending to the crying baby and her husband blamed her for this. Shripati, the husband stopped speaking to his wife, he has not spoken to her since the day it happened about thirty-five years ago. Her daughter Sumi recognises the great contribution of this self-punishing woman, "Infact, noticing the complex net of relationship that Kalyani has with so many people, Sumi is reminded of the spider she had seen one morning, scuttling from point to point, drawing silken threads out of it, and weaving in the process a web with a beautiful design."[18] Kalyani is visibly upset when she comes to know about Gopal's walking away on his wife and children. She will never like the tragedy of her life to resurface in the case of her daughter. She cries, "No, no, my God, not again" pathetically, "sounding so much like an animal in pain." [(MT, 12)] When she goes to meet Gopal, she pleads him not to let it happen to Sumi what had happened to her. She takes the entire responsibility of Sumi's carelessness on herself. She says: "But ..... how could she have known what being a good wife means? when she never saw her mother being one? I taught her nothing, it's my fault, Gopala, forgive me and don't punish her for it." [(MT, 47)] It clearly shows her disappointment as a mother. She is very much affected at the loss of her son and that is why she can't bear the pain of her daughter again even as her married life comes to an end, with the loss of this mentally retarded son. She is also secluded in her pain. Some other mother figures in the novel *Roots and Shadows*, are Indu's aunt Atya and Sunanda. Though they are quite different from each other, they represent two faces of the same coin – the courage of women and deviousness of women. While Atya displays strength and courage in her oppressed circumstances, Sunanda reveals the deviousness of a woman in a patriarchy who manipulates circumstances to suit herself in order to exist. Atya, Indu's aunt, is sixty years old childless widow and dependent on her natal family. She is one of those traditional women who remain unfazed by misfortunes. One of the principal merits of the joint family has been that it provides support to women who have no means of livelihood. Atya is one such woman. Unlike Akka, she has played the surrogate mother, devoted to tending the members of the old house selflessly, and giving them her undemanding affection. By contrast, there is Sunanda Atya's younger sister who is portrayed as cunning and manipulative. If women can dominate, women can also be vulnerable. Shashi Deshpande's fiction presents the second aspect in the character of Kusum and Mohan's mother in *That Long Silence,* and Mira, Kishore's mother, in *The Binding Vine.* Both Kusum and Mohan's mother lack the strength to fight the oppressive social set up in which they live. Their social position makes it impossible for them even to vent their resentment upon other women. The character of Kusum seems significant only in so far as it highlights Jaya's own predicament. Shashi Deshpande also employs Kusum's character to illustrate the helplessness of the traditional woman who, unable to give a voice to her suppressed self, turns her aggression upon herself. Jaya's sweeper Nayana in *That Long Silence*, represents the typical lower class Indian mother. She continues to get pregnant in the hope of giving birth to a male child. Notwithstanding her obviously patriarchal desire for a son, she is protective and caring towards her daughters because she knows that a fate similar to her is in store for them when they grow up. Her attitude reveals both the passive acceptance by women of the dominant patriarchal values and also her adjustment to them.

The halo around motherhood is clearly missing in Shashi Deshpande's novels. The modern and educated mothers do not pose to be the serenc Madomma figures, clasping their children to their bosom. What with relinquishing the halo of motherhood, as a mother claims Jaya has done, neither she nor Saru can relinquish their motherly love. Saru constantly thinks of her children and their little needs when she is away sending them off to school, keeping them warm at night. But In spite of all these things she failed as a mother. She cannot communicate about her problems to her children. Similarly, Jaya thinks of Rati and Rahul and is ever worried for their welfare. Both, Saru and Jaya at times, show gender bias despite their being enlightened which is vociferously resented by Rati and Renu.

The mother daughter relationship has always occupied an important place in Shashi Deshpande's novels. Her portrayal of the mother also seems to be a reaction to the idealised depiction of the mother and motherhood in mythology and other Indian literature. She wants to depict woman as an individual rather than as cast in a particular mould or role.

## Notes and References

1. Usha Bande. *Mothers And Mother-Figures in Indo-English Literature,* (Jalandhar: ABS Publications, 1994), 1.

2. K.C. Baral. "Reading The Mother: Psychoanalysis and Indian Novel Written in English", ed. by. Usha Bande, *Mothers and Mother-Figures in Indo-English Literature,* 1994, 16.
3. Jasbir Jain. *Gendered Realities, Human Spaces, the Writing of Shashi Deshpande,* (Jaipur: Rawat Publications, 2003), 57.
4. Sarbjit K. Sandhu. *The Image of Woman in The Novels of Shashi Deshpande,* (New Delhi: Prestige Books, 1991), 19-20.
5. Ragini Ramachandra. "Rev. of The Dark Holds No Terrors, *The Literary Criterion,* Vol. XXI, Nos. I & 2, 1986, 120.
6. Shashi Deshpande. *The Dark Holds No Terrors,* (New Delhi: Penguin Books, 1990), 45, here after cited in the chapter.
7. Rashmi Sahi. "Human Relationship in the Novels of Shashi Deshpande", *Indian Literature,* Vol.42, No.4, July – Aug 1998, 168.
8. Mrinalini Sebestian. *The Novels of Shashi Deshpande In Postcolonial Arguments,* (New Delhi: Sangam Books, 2000), 176-177.
9. Basavraj Naikar. "Joys And Sorrows of Womanhood in The Binding Vine", ed. by, Suman Bala, (New Delhi: Khosla Publishing House, 2001), 123.
10. Siddhartha Sharma. *Shashi Deshpande's Novels: A Feminist Study,* (New Delhi: Atlantic Publishers and Distributors, 2005), 48.
11. Shashi Deshpande. *The Binding Vine,* (New Delhi: Penguin Books, 1993), 58. here after cited in the chapter.
12. Gowri Sivaraman. "Self-Pitying Specimens Emerging as Self-Confident Neophytes in Some Writings of Shashi Deshpande",
13. Shashi Deshpande. *That Long Silence,* (London: Virgo Press, 1988), 61-62, here after cited in the chapter.
14. S. Indira. "A Bond or Burden? A Study of Shashi Deshpande's The Binding Vine," *Indian Women Novelists,* Set III, Vol.6, ed. R.K. Dhawan, (New Delhi: Prestige, 1995), 22.
15. Shashi Deshpande. *Small Remedies,* (New Delhi: Viking, Penguin, 2000), 303, here after cited in the chapter.
16. Ranjini Jyothi Singh. "Quest For Space and Selfhood In Shashi Deshpande's Small Remedies", *Pegasus,* Vol.4, Jan-Dec 2005, 22.
17. Shashi Deshpande. *Moving On,* (New Delhi: Penguin Books, 2004), 61, here after cited in the chapter.
18. Shashi Deshpande. *A Matter of Time,* (New Delhi: Penguin Books, 1996), 12, here after cited in the chapter.

## CHAPTER 5

# Revolt

Shashi Deshpande's novels are concerned with a woman's quest for self; an exploration into the female psyche and an understanding of the mysteries of life and the protagonists place in it. Through the centuries, Indian woman has tried to create her own space within a patriarchal society which regards her as primarily an adjunct to a man. Women have ruled vast households. Women have found voices in music, art and literature and yet, by and large, they have unquestioningly accepted their subaltern position in society. The vast majority has regarded that position as inevitable, almost destined; they have interiorised the dominating patriarchal ideology so thoroughly that there was no scope for a critical re-evaluation of either the norms of society or of their own needs for self-fulfillment.

The Indian woman of the twentieth century is placed in a rather different and more complex situation. The Indian social environment has felt the impact of modernisation, education, and the mass media. Economic compulsions have led to a significant widening of the horizons of a woman's life without a corresponding re-definition of social values, placing her proverbially speaking, in the horns of a dilemma. According to Anuradha Roy: "Educated, enlightened, demanding more from herself and life than her predecessors, conscious of an identity apart from that which links her to a male, she is yet faced by numerous age-old assumptions about the temperament she is expected to possess, the attitudes to be displayed, and the role to be played"[1]. Woman's experiences, her dilemmas are an epitome of an uneasy transitional phase through which Indian society is re-defining itself in keeping with the changing times. Her outlook broadened through education and a greater exposure to the outside world, she has to confront many demons, both external and internal which still demand from her an unswerving allegiance to an ideal of womanhood forged through centuries of patriarchal impositions. But she has perforce to examine and re-evaluate what her predecessors had accepted as unchangeable and incontrovertibly right. In an article on the need to decode gender consciousness in texts, Sukrita Paul Kumar makes an interesting and pertinent point. She refers to Elaine Showalter's well-known differentiation of feminist consciousness into three separate phases – "the feminine phase of internalisation, the feminist phase of revolt and the female phase of self-discovery."[3] She points out that in the Indian context: "there is no such historical linearity; what is witnessed here is the simultaneous existence of all three. A long cultural history diverse live mythology combined with a fairly long exposure to western education lends a strange complexity to the modes of existence here." (AR, 71)

Shashi Deshpande's aim has also been to depict and analyse the Indian woman, her dilemmas, and conflicts against the background of coeval Indian. She has made use of her life experiences, and her works continue to make significant contribution to Indian writing in English. The issues and themes in her novels arise from the situation of woman at the crossroads of a transitional society, changing from traditional to modern. This chapter explores the complexity of contemporary existence where woman is precariously poised between two worlds, one which she cannot totally reject and the other which she cannot easily accept. This is a vital phase in the evolution of a feminist consciousness in the protagonist. An increasing awareness that patriarchal forces are defacing her identity is now combined with a growing refusal to surrender to such forces.

Dr. N. Sethuraman observes: "Woman in Shashi Deshpande's novels establish herself as an independent being, free from the restrictions imposed by society, culture, and also from their own fears and guilt. The vital insight that Shashi Deshpande brings to the readers is that woman should accept her own responsibility for what they are and see how much she has contributed to her own victimisation."[4] She is primarily concerned with the woman and her eternal quest for life. She has tried to project a realistic picture of the middle class educated women who are financially independent and represent a large part of the contemporary Indian society. Her novels mostly deal with the problems of adjustments and dilemmas in the minds of a female protagonist and ultimately, they endeavour to submit to the traditional rules in transitional society. A tradition bound woman may sacrifice her happiness for the sake of the well-being of the family as a unit, but at the same time retains her individuality. Indian woman usually does not bother about her own personal happiness and comfort as much as she addresses herself to the task of making others happy and upholding traditions and conventions. A woman may be seen and understood by her father in one way, her husband in another way, her son and daughter in some other ways and by herself in yet another way. Shashi Deshpande's novels present a social world of many complex relationships. Many men and women live together and journey across life in their different age groups, classes, and gendered roles. Doubt, anxiety and often a feeling of void of values push characters, in her novels, to intense self-examination. The woman is particularly caught in the process of redefining and rediscovering her own role, position, and relationship within her given social world. She presents the modern Indian womanhood in her novels. Her own struggle as a writer to focus on women's issues, dilemmas and experience is equally symptomatic of the resistance to feminist expression that prevails in India in the middle of twentieth century. As a woman writer, her dilemma was either to give voice to women's concern and be branded as a woman writer; removed from the mainstream of literary scene, or to deny her femininity and write like a man either with the male name or male narrative voices. The live experiences and viewpoint of woman represent after all one half of humanity. Her emphatic claim that she is feminist came gradually to her as her main literary concern. The concerns of woman are primarily in the context of the family and the community. Shashi Deshpande has looked into woman's changing perspectives and her search for bonding within family as a mode of strength. The novelist uses this point of view to present social reality as it is experienced by women. To present the world of mothers, daughters, and wives, she also presents indirectly the fathers, sons and husbands, the relation between man and woman, and between women themselves. According to N.B. Masal, "In presenting woman's point of view, Shashi Deshpande is mainly interested in the clash of tradition and modernity, as reflected in the generation gap and conflict between women. Her young heroines revolt against the traditional way of life and patriarchal values. Jaya, Sarita and Sumi perceive the structuring of men and women in gendered roles, restricting their human potentiality and fullness. They struggle to transcend the restrictive roles. They revolt, reject and seek freedom from the traditional norms and way of life."[5]

The woman in the novels of Shashi Deshpande, in order to achieve her freedom seeks marriage as an alternative to the bondage created by the parental family. The simple need to be independent eventually becomes a demand of the inflated ego and takes shape as the love for power over others. She resents the role of a daughter and looks forward to the role of a wife with the hope that her new role will help her in winning her freedom. As Prasanna Sree Sathupati observes: "The parental home symbol of tradition and old-world values has no room for Shashi Deshpande's women, for they breathe the air of rituals that obstruct the growth of a woman as a being."[6] Indu and Saru seek freedom through marriage, a room of their own and autonomy. The woman, in order to achieve her freedom seeks marriage as an alternative to the bondage created by the parental family. She resents the role as a daughter and looks forward to the role as a wife, with the hope that her new role will help her in winning her freedom. Saru's situation is explicitly described in the novel: "I had come away from my parents in a fever of excitement after the last battle. The die was cast, the decisions taken, my boats burnt. There could be no turning back. Then, this ridiculous anticlimax."[6]

Saru in *The Dark Holds No Terror*, hails from a tradition bound family which leaves scars on her psyche. Sharing the similar backdrop as that of Indu, Saru has no love lost for her family, especially her mother. Treated as a second-rate citizen in her own home, owing to gender discrimination, she develops a deep and severe hatred towards her mother. The sibling rivalry between herself and her brother Dhruv verges almost on the unnatural. "He is different. He's a boy," these words establish the tradition bound Indian mother against whom Saru has to rebel all through her life. Her impotent anger makes her rage against her mother: "If you are a woman, I don't want to be one."[7] Saru goes against her family and joins medical profession. It is once again against the wishes of her mother that she marries Manohar, a man of her choice. The departure of the protagonist from the mother is the first step towards autonomy. Defiance seems to be the second nature to Saru. She defies her mother to become a doctor, defies her caste to marry outside, and defies social conventions by using Boozie to advance her career. To her chagrin, Saru realises that her marriage to Manu, instead of promised freedom, led her once again into unwanted bondage. Saru's success as a doctor leads to the discord in her marriage and disintegration in her relationship with Manu. Saru's success breeds insecurity in Manu and Saru recognises the fact: Now I know that it was there it began….. this terrible thing that has destroyed our marriage." (DHNT, 37) Intolerable as he is of Saru's importance in the role of a doctor, yet he cannot ask her to give it up. The material comforts he hesitates to do without. Instead, he tries to soothe his male ego by physically asserting himself over her. His transformation from a doting husband into a sadist invokes terror in the heart of Saru and she comes to detest the very word love: "Love… how I scorned the word." (DHNT, 65) Despite her hatred of Manu's physical sadism Saru refuses to take any action and loathes to admit failure. Saru refrains herself from announcing it to the world that her marriage has been a failure. She admits: "I have been clinging to the tenuous shadow of a marriage whose substance has long since disintegrated, because I have been afraid of proving my mother right." (DHNT, 179) She confesses further that she had come away from her parents in a fever of excitement after the last battle. The die was cast, the decision taken, her boats burnt. There could be no turning back. Saru returns to her parental home only to experience her mother's total rejection of herself. She admits defeat: "she had gone, leaving the battle unfinished, taking victory away with herself." (DHNT, 153) Nevertheless she is racked by a terrible feeling of guilt: "There can never be any forgiveness. Never any atonement. My brother died because I heedlessly turned my back on him. My mother died alone because I deserted her. My husband is a failure because I destroyed his manhood." (DHNT, 198)

It is in order to get away from the mother who accused her of having murdered her brother that Saru marries defiantly. But even this supposition turns out to be nothing but a mirage. Undecided about her stance as a woman, Saru returns to her family house. Even the parental home does not provide the required refuge. Instead of feeling overjoyed of being home, she feels enclosed. She even fails to relate to her father: "As she drinks her tea…. too sweet and strong…. He (father) sat gingerly on the edge of his chair like an unwilling host entertaining an unwelcome guest. And that I suppose is what I really am. What gave me the idea that I could come back? (DHNT, 14)

Saru's feeling of homelessness is an affirmation of her sense of seclusion. Saru leaves home twice in the novel to seek release, once to establish her independence from mother's suppression and the second time to establish her indispensability to her husband and children. When victimized by Manu, she starts on a quest for home and reaches the home she had earlier rejected, "Home is the place where, when you have to go there, they have to take you in. It (Manu's house) was not home. Nor was this (father's house) home. How odd, to live for so long and discover that you have no home at all!" (DHNT, 155)

The home-hunt is in essence a peace-hunt. Home is what one makes of any house. Saru could once make a happy home of just a room with Manu. It was a time when the external world did not matter at all to them, and it is not healthy to live in seclusion. How they can relate to the external world and yet be an organic unit is what home is all about. One has to be at peace with oneself, to be at peace with others. Despite her driving need for a stretching hand, a comforting touch, Saru refuses to be let down by the feeling of seclusion and aloneness. She takes stock of herself: "All right, so I'm alone. But so's everyone else. Human beings….. they're going to fail you. But because there's just us, because there's no one else, we have to go on trying. If we can't believe in ourselves, we're sunk." (DHNT, 200)

Despite seclusion, man can seek a meaningful life in human interdependence too. Saru's need for a confidant and her finding some relief in unburdening her heart to the father, reiterates the idea of interdependence. The perfect partnership between Madhav and the father is a demonstration of the meaningful interdependence. It is a perfect pattern where they make no demand to each other.

Suddenly it comes to her that neither Manu nor her father can be her refuge. She has to seek her own refuge and find her true self. This journey into herself, this self-exploration (search for identity) reveals her that she has to be at peace with herself before achieving anything. She decides not to pretend and struggle anymore as it only brings solace and loneliness. Integrity is the key to wholeness and this she realises: "The guilty sister, the undutiful wife…. all persons spiked with guilt. Yes, she was all of them, she would not deny that now. She had to accept these selves to become whole again. But if she was all of them, they were not all of her. She was all that and so much more." (DHNT, 207)

Learning truth by oneself is the first step towards autonomy and Saru is able to achieve this. Her earlier doubts as to retaining her professional integrity as a doctor evaporate in thin air as she tends, confidently, to Sunita's illness. She tells her father: "And oh yes, Baba, if Manu comes, tell him to wait. I'll be back as soon as I can." (DHNT,

202) With this self-realisation occurs the tacit understanding that any meaningful relationship is interdependent. Integration alone would make her whole again and confrontation of the disintegrating elements alone would make that possible. Escapism is no permanent solution, nor should one look to anything outside of oneself to provide the solution but seek it within.

The title of the novel effectively presents the need for confrontation in terms of light and darkness. Saru's caution to Dhruv – "the dark holds no terrors. That the terrors are inside us all the time. We carry them with in us, and like traitors, they spring out when we least expect them, to scratch and maul," (DHNT, 76-77) is what she needs to apply to herself.

The backdrop of Shashi Deshpande's novels has been prepared by women who are victims of such pathogenic misogyny. These women have suffered the atrocities of men in silence and without protest, as they were not aware of protest as an option to change their world. Their inner turmoil, flabbergasted emotional resilience and relational bondage has been suggestively juxtaposed against the desperate struggle of her protagonists to define and obtain a self-hood, thus putting it in a sustained and sharpened focus to indicate the changing dynamics of man-woman relation. Jaya in *That Long Silence* confronts her own enslavement to an image of an ideal wife. She is deprived of even wholeness. Ensconced in the structures and prescriptions of security, acculturate firmly into socially determined roles and attitudes, Jaya the narrator protagonist is confronted with the basic problem of fixing her identity, of recovering the self from the roles of dutiful daughter, submissive wife, and caring mother. Jaya rejects the very idea of a unitary self. She is a credible and moving embodiment of the modern Indian woman seeing for an honest understanding of her. Sarla Palkar observes, "*That Long Silence,* is also a self-critique. The important insight that Shashi Deshpande imparts to us through Jaya is that women should accept their own responsibility for what they are, see how much they have contributed to their own victimisation, instead of putting the blame on everybody except themselves."[8] The novel represents a constructive attempt at the re-definition of a woman's selfhood in an environment where age old patriarchal assumptions clash with liberal ideas of individuation. The confrontation with the truth of her is a painful process, involving a prolonged phase of intense introspection. As the veneer of the self, she has created at the dictates of social norms cracks, Jaya undergoes a crisis of recriminations and self-admonishment; she passes through a bitter realisation of constraints, disenchantment, and self-deprecation to a courageous and fair proportioning of responsibility which does not ignore her own culpability. What emerges from one woman's attempt to re-discover her sense of identity is ultimately a scathing critique of our social institutions like marriage or family.

The protagonist Jaya is caught in the midst of a domestic storm. Her husband is accused of corrupt practices at office and the couple leaves their posh flat at Bombay's Church Gate to an Old Dadar flat of theirs. The children go out on a holiday. That gives space to Jaya for self-interrogation. Traditionally, a woman has an identity only as husband's wife or father's daughter or son's mother. The real picture, the real you, never emerges. Looking for it is as bewildering as trying to know you really look. Ten different mirrors show ten different faces. The individuality of Jaya cannot be defined. She can be defined only in relation to others. That woman is always defined and differentiated with reference to man and not he with the reference to her, is true of the Indian women in spite of legislations and many safeguards provided. Shashi Deshpande is aware of many constraints present in the Indian society and she defines freedom for Indian women from the point of view of the Indian society. Jaya was aware of an inner void, hollowness in her life, even though it was shielded by the deceptively beautiful screen of her social graces and obligations. Her stream of consciousness makes it clear that even in the educated upper middle classes the intrinsic value of intelligent and capable woman is invariably affected by her social status, since society treats her as an object or a possession – never as an individual. There are moments for Jaya when social and familial responsibilities do not remain a pleasure but become a bondage, because she is forced to accept these compulsively as a female. Her married life forces her to put herself on exhibition, but it did not enable her to understand herself successfully. Instead of taking her out of her seclusion, it confirms her seclusion from the personal and the social worlds. Her inability to establish a normal relationship with her husband enhances her frustration. However, she overcomes the barrier of this unnatural silence after a bitter struggle and realises that negation of one's emotional needs never leads a woman towards self-hood. An understanding of one's motives, accepting responsibilities for one's decisions and clear bilateral communication of priorities and decisions is required to obtain peace, harmony, and fulfillment in life. Marital relationships have almost inevitably been the focal point of novels written by Shashi Deshpande. The emphasis is not on the development or mechanics of the relationship but on the forces which work together to make the relationship a farcical exhibition of togetherness. Functioning along fixed parameters, marriages become an arid formality, devoid of contact. With her new self-awareness, Jaya ironically views herself and Mohan "as a pair of bullocks yoked together moving together merely because it was more comfortable".[9] And also "a husband is like a sheltering tree, her aunt had told her, leaving her to make the logical inferences that since the tree afforded shelter and protection, "You have to keep the tree alive and flourishing, even if you have to water it with deceit and lies." (TLS, 32) But a cynical thought flash through Jaya's mind; she is reminded of a creeper which had been assiduously cared for but had died, perhaps of too much water. Too much care and too little of spontaneity could be equally harmful to a marriage. Marriage was the only career she had and in order to make a success of it, she had lost herself and become the male construct of an ideal wife. A sense of non-fulfillment, of incompleteness, had lain dormant in Jaya for years, suppressed out of fear of denting the facade of a happy marriage. Silence is, perhaps, the most common strategy of survival. The silences of the novel are not those of peace and tranquility. Rather, they are an amalgam of pain, anger, defensiveness, and rejection. Silence takes various shapes in the novel, ranging from Mohan's mother's silence of absolute despair to the resigned silence of Vimala who impassively bleeds to death, the unthinking silence of Kusum as she slowly sinks into insanity, the stoic silence of the maid Jeeja, whose sole purpose in life was to go on living. But Jaya has the potential to speak out, to revolt against the silence thrust on her by the tradition-ridden society; however, she is conscious of the never-ending game a woman plays till the end of her life. Jaya, with a mind of her own struggling to assert itself against the suffocating effect of cultural mores has, however, gone beyond such resigned acceptance. Her silence is one bristling with suppressed anger and a strong sense of injustice. Jaya had been silent when Mohan had excused his irregular financial dealings with "I did it for you," (TLS, 10) silent when he had taken umbrage at the story of which she had been so proud, in silence bearing the burden of wifehood. When the inevitable outburst does take place, the simmering anger and resentment at last finds expression as Jaya and Mohan trade accusations, until finally Mohan stomps off, leaving Jaya to re-appraise her marriage in these frighteningly new circumstances. The new crisis and the breaking of the bondage of silence will ultimately lead to a redeemed marriage based on stronger foundations. Soon after marriage Jaya had her first and only outburst against her husband. Mohan remained silent for some days after that Jaya had learnt to become silent too. She reconciled with Mohan even as she kept her grouse with her. Mohan had taken notes from code of conduct for married women, "my mother never raised her voice against my father, however badly he behaved to her." (TLS, 83) There is an instance when the gravity of the situation weighs against her silence. She tells herself, "I must not laugh, I must not laugh." (TLS, 122) But she laughed hysterically when Mohan, involved in a bribery case and was on the verge of facing prosecution and dismissal from job, fiercely accuses her of all his misadventures. The hysterical laughs land her in an awkward and despairing situation. Jaya experiences the torture of seclusion and long silence when her hysterical laughter makes Mohan desert her. She reverts to the firm hold of marriage that has crushed her soul in the past. *That Long Silence*, at last breaks with her story fully narrated and all her anguish articulated. The process of self-discovery is illuminating, and it is a cathartic experiment. It is a rebirth and a resurrection of self. A new Jaya is born out of an agonising and despairing Jaya. She pledges to live a whole life retaining all that did not fit in the strait jacket of wifehood. She decided to give her own answers to Mohan, not the answers expected by him. Shashi Deshpande is in the quest of creating new woman out of her protagonists who belong to different cultural, religious, and linguistic backgrounds. Jaya realises that in order to attain self-hood, a woman must transcend silence, negation, and self-alienation. A woman's relation with her family must burgeon with in the totality of her life as a woman. Only then it can lead to a harmonious fulfillment. She realises that a holistic yet resilient approach towards life is necessary, "we don't change overnight. It's possible that we may not change even over long periods of time, but we can always hope. Without that, life would be impossible. And if there is anything to know now it is this: life has always to be made possible." (TLS, 193) Her decision to cease to be a passive partner and overcome the turbulence in her relationship with Mohan leads her to uninhibited self-identification.

The novel clearly spells out the faith that a woman's desire to succeed like an individual does not negate or cancel her desire for love, marriage and domesticity. A balanced and purposeful life is not a utopian fancy for a woman if she liberates herself from the stereotyped conditioning of society and is not dependent on the male presence to authenticate her thoughts, emotions, and deeds at every step. *That Long Silence* aesthetically communicates the essence of the creed of feminism along with the contemporary realities. Central to *That Long Silence*, is an attempt by Jaya to liberate herself from the prescribed and interiorised role of the other, an adjunct to her husband, and find her own identity as a human being capable of thinking and acting on her own initiative. In the days that she spends alone in the flat after Mohan walks out in a fit of anger, Jaya has the opportunity to confront suppressed truth about herself as not merely a wife, but as a writer, a mother, a friend, a woman capable of strong physical urges. If the creation of a common female experience is one of the hallmarks of feminist fiction, *That Long Silence*, can undoubtedly claim to belong to the category. Shashi Deshpande uses Jaya's path to a constructive resolution to articulate the dilemma of the educated middle-class Indian woman. The unpretentious realism of presentation gives these experiences a representational quality. The process of Jaya's self-definition draws into it many significant issues concerning women's existence in a changing society – the issues of women's writing, female sexuality, motherhood, wifehood, and the necessity of discarding silence as a strategy of survival.

Of the novels examined in this study, *That Long Silence*, is the only one to explore the problems of female self-expression through a career. In a world slowly opening outdoors of opportunity to women, the urge to extend themselves beyond the confines of domesticity is very real for many educated women. Saru in *The Dark Holds No Terrors,* and Indu in *Roots and Shadows,* are on the surface, successful emancipated women with fulfilling careers; Shashi Deshpande shows that in reality, they have not yet emotionally extricated themselves from patriarchal impositions, both direct and indirect. Obsessed as she is by the role of ideal homemaker and self-sacrificing wife, Jaya has yet attempted to create a space for herself through her writing. Jaya's attempt to find her own voice as a writer is turned into a significant depiction of the forces – external and internal conditioning the whole process of women's writing.

Jaya's decision to break the bondage of silence carries with it a confident hope for change. The process of introspection and articulation through her writing has given the courage to speak out, to reject her earlier image of herself and Mohan as a pair of bullocks yoked for life, to admit the possibility of change, to make life possible.

Shashi Deshpande's heroines reject rituals that are vestiges of the past. Indu in *Roots and Shadows*, wanted to explore the inner struggle of her. She represents a set of the modern women who are educated and are very much in contact with the society, dealing with the critical problems like love, sex marriage, settlement, and individuality. Indu reviews everything with reason. She analyses the ideals of detachment and freedom and tries to achieve them. She tries to listen to the voice of her conscience and revolts. Indu is projected against the women belonging to the older generation. To an old generation, a woman's life is nothing but to get married, to bear children, to have sons and then grandchildren and the ideal woman is the one who does not have her own independent identity. Indu wanted to protest against these conventional laws which are moulding the female character as only symbols of lust. In *Roots and Shadows*, Indu too searches for release from the constraints of the tradition-bound institution of marriage in search of an autonomous self. The realisation of the need to conform for survival and the awareness that conformity is the great destroyer of selfhood, and the only self that can be achieved is the self-born in interpersonal relationship make Indu cry: "This is my real sorrow that I can never be complete in myself, there was somewhere outside me a part of me without which I remained complete, then I met Jayant, and lost the ability to be alone."[10]

Highly sensitive, intelligent, and educated Indu could be said to be a representative of modern young woman. Indu, a middle-class young girl, brought up in an orthodox Brahmin family, headed by Akka, the mother surrogate in the novel, left home full of hatred for the family, for Akka specially and she had sworn never to go back. Indu, who had lost her mother at birth, identifies throughout the novel, Akka as the mother figure. She revolts against Akka, her world, her values and marries Jayant against the wishes of Akka. In marrying Jayant, Indu had thought that she had found her alter ego – had found in him a spiritual and psychological level of closeness. But marriage with Jayant had forced her to realise that self is an elusive centre that one could never exchange roots with another that this was an illusion and she felt cheated. Losing her own identity and living in the wake of her husband troubles her enormously. She does not find herself modern young woman any different from her mother. There is no doubt that she loves Jayant and wants him by her side at all times. But the self-same love seems to be shackling her to his side and is preventing her from taking stock of her as a separate entity: "What I feel for Jayant ...... Can I compress all of it within this world? It is much more, so overwhelming a response of the whole of me to him. Sometimes I wonder if I will love him one day and live by myself. The only way in which I can be myself, my whole self again." (RS, 97)

Unable to come to terms with either her love for Jayant or her true self, Indu finds herself stifled and suppressed. Her marriage, she finds, is robbing her of her identity as a person apart and separating from her husband. Feeling entrapped yet she hesitates to come out of her entanglements. Her realisation that she too is being moulded into the very image of woman she tried to break away from, worries her. In the first place she has broken from her family because she wanted to prove herself to be as different and as unlike as possible from women like Akka. It is her sole reason for her rebelling against the family norms and marrying Jayant. But marriage to Jayant does not prove to be the heaven she hopes for and dreams of. Even in her professional life, she is expected to curtail her freedom and submit to the demands of her editor, and thus indirectly to the society. Her return to her parental home comes as a revelation to Indu. The feeling of homelessness is indicative of inner disintegration. Tension between the different parts with in one's self takes away the harmony within and without. The novel gains its feminist stance in Indu's exploration into herself, but it also moves beyond the boundaries of feminism into a perception of the very predicament of the human existence. Indu moves on the road of self-realisation and the destination seems to be the point of comprehension of the mystery of human life. Shashi Deshpande suggests that Indu has learnt to see not only her life full of possibilities for growth and grace, but the very meeting of life itself. At the end of the novel Indu realises that Akka is not as sadist as thought earlier, Indu has confronted her real self and she knows her roots.

The women in *Roots and Shadows*, and *The Dark Holds No Terrors,* do not present themselves as the women who want to go in self-quest, and are free from the restrictions imposed by society, culture, nature and are also free from their own fear and guilt. Commenting on *Roots and Shadows*, O.P. Bhatnagar remarks: "The novel deals with a woman's attempt to assert her individuality and realise her freedom. It depicts how it brings her into confrontation with family, with male-dominated society."[11] Indu's struggle for selfhood, her struggle towards liberation of the mind, her struggle for an emotional and intellectual definition of herself as a self – actualising person, is in a sense to fight against her womanhood. Fullness of experience for a woman in a tradition – bound society is used to look upon marriage as woman's ultimate destiny, as an assertion of her womanhood. How to reconcile woman's human demand for freedom with her need for love and how to strike a balance between her wifehood, motherhood and career and spiritual fulfillment are some of the issues raised by Shashi Deshpande in *Roots and Shadows*. Indu refuses to be the mother of a child that is not wholly welcome in a marriage that has become non-real because love is non-real in a marriage and that, therefore, makes her feel trapped in a negative situation since it threatens her positive struggle for independence, for selfhood, and her effort at intellectual liberation.

Indu's dilemma expresses Shashi Deshpande's feminist policies against gender roles imposed upon women in a patriarchal culture. Ever ready to please Jayant, Indu acquiesces to his desires. Indu gradually realises that she does not exist for her but for Jayant, the archetypal male, imperialistic and subjugating. She feels in her a sense of existential insecurity, but she ultimately realises that she has been chasing shadows, leaving her roots far behind in the family and in Jayant too. Naren, with whom she develops an adulterous relationship, is nothing more than a mere shadow to her. He has no permanent place in her memory. Hence, she decides to go back to Jayant. She feels that it is she who is to be blamed for the marital discord in their lives. She has created a hell out of a heaven. She realises that marriage had stunted and hampered her individuality because she had regarded it as a trap and not as a bond. She realises that each time, she had cut off some part of her real self to please Jayant, but this had turned their marriage into a farce. Thus, Indu's uncompromising and paradoxical feminine self that frantically longed for self-expression, finally finds its roots in the home and with her husband. Shadows disappear from her vision, and she sees the clear light of day with the realisation and discovery of her identity. The meek, docile, and humble Indu of the early days finally emerges as a bold, challenging, conscious and rebellious woman. She resigns her job, thus defying the male authority, hierarchy, and the irony of a woman's masked existence. Her self-discovery is the frightening visions of the feminine self's struggle for harmony and sanity. She comes out of her emotional upheaval and decides to lead a meaningful life with her husband. The home she had discarded becomes the place of refuge, of solace and consolation. It is Akka's house which offers her ample opportunities to know herself. It is here that she is able to discover her roots as an independent woman, as a daughter, as a mother and as a commercial writer. The end of the novel sees a new Indu – determined, free and always in search to make her marriage work, but on new terms. She decides to spend the money; Akka has left her the way she wants and not according to other people's wishes. She finds personal freedom and completeness. Indu now takes matters into her own hands; she faces the fact of her own fault in her problems with Jayant. She will now try to save her marriage, but without compromising her principles or her individuality. Through the character of Indu, Shashi Deshpande has represented the new woman who is aware of her situation, her quest, her identity, her place and her role in the family and in society.

In portraying the various women characters, Shashi Deshpande shows that they seek fulfillment only within the orbit of family and relationships. *The Binding Vine* explores important problems of our time without offering any facile solutions. Shashi Deshpande's protagonists may be independent to some extent but are firmly bound by the shackles of tradition. Urmila, perhaps, is the most rebellious of Shashi Deshpande's women characters. Unlike the protagonists in the other novels written by her, who are aware of the inequalities in society but do not attempt to set right anything, Urmila takes up cudgels on behalf of a rape victim, Kalpana. She is instrumental in publicising the case and getting the police to investigate the matter and find the culprit. She encourages her friend, Vanaa, to assert herself and stop behaving like a door mat. She also sets herself to the task of translating the poems written by her mother-in-law in Kannada to English and intends publishing them. Shashi Deshpande's clarion call to modern women in this novel is loud and clear. The patriarchal, chauvinistic, and indifferent Indian male role is challenged. The inner most recesses of a woman's heart are brought to light through the perspective, of the protagonist,

Urmi. Death of a second child forms the occasion for a journey into the past, into oneself and into the future. The experience is one which minutely analyses all the relationships a woman in the Indian society is subjected to. There are moments of revolt, deep felt anger, desire to set things right, retreat from steps which would shatter the sense of well-being and fulfillment mirrored through these relationships. The final resolution is one which points at a relationship that is healthy, satisfying, something that is based on love and the wish to help, rather than drown the soul into the quagmire of the dark night. All this has prompted Indira Nityanandam to write: "The Binding Vine, is a refreshing change from the first three novels of Shashi Deshpande. Protest comes easily to her protagonist here and there is less agony in attempting to change societal roles and attitudes. The hope for Indian women lies in the happy fact that though there are Miras and Kalpanas and Shakutai's, we also have our Urmilas."[12] The narrator is a woman, and it is mainly the woman's perspective that is presented in the novel. The keynote of the novel is struck right at the beginning where Urmi determines not to be plaster cast into a stereotyped image by people around her. If an accidental fall from a cycle and the consequent injury and anxiety make her feel a restriction in her freedom, an existential experience such as death plunges her into morbidity and a masochistic mood which is devoid of all positive values. The gradual progress of the self through darkness, revolt and reconciliation is what is traced through a narration of Urmi's experience. The past, secure in Urmi's grandmother Baiajji's company, is a panorama of solidarity and orientation. This past comes to an end leading to a present, where the central character feels trapped without exits and escapes. Urmi is, without links, suspicious of all and stubborn in her seclusion and emptiness. The female consciousness has suffered during the moments ushered in by external events such as death or rape, and such experiences suppress her into the quicksand of traditional and submissive roles, but it is the emergence of the modern woman, individualistic and confident that is finally achieved. The two central ideas that lead the protagonist into an analysis of women's issues are death and rape.

Shashi Deshpande's protagonists often end up discovering good traits in people whom they had earlier dismissed as selfish or cruel. Similarly, they also discover the seamy side of those whom they had all along taken as angels of love or fair play. Shashi Deshpande does not believe in portraying her characters in black and white. After their circuitous journey through life and marriage, her protagonists, who have started their journey from their parental homes in search of the freedom of the self, come to realise.

In presenting women's point of view, Shashi Deshpande is mainly interested in the clash of tradition and modernity, as reflected in the generation gap and conflicts between women. Her young protagonists revolt against the traditional way of life and patriarchal values. Jaya, Sarita, Indu and Sumi perceive the structuring of men and women in gendered roles, restricting their human potentiality and fullness. They struggle to transcend the restrictive roles. They rebel, reject and seek freedom from the traditional norms and way of life. If the bonds that bind human life help individuals in continuing their lives despite the betrayals and cruelties associated with human survival, everybody has a life of one's own to live. So is also for Sumi in *A Matter of Time*. She is different from Indu, Saru, Jaya and Urmila – the women protagonists of Shashi Deshpande's earlier novels. Sumi evolves herself from the utter desolation and bitterness linked up with invisible chains of patriarchal pressure and other family responsibilities. She is seen gradually emancipating herself as a new and independent woman. Gopal's desertion makes her experience the trauma of a deserted wife and the anguish of a secluded partner. All the agonies and dilemmas of life corner her at the age of forty and make her stand alone and helpless along with her teenaged daughters Aru, Charu, and Seema. Generally, on being deserted, a woman seems to be emotionally shattered. But Sumi is not emotionally broken. On the other hand, like any responsible mother, Sumi helps her children to get on with their lives as before. If Indu and Saru seek refuge at their parental homes and Jaya at her Dadar flat, Sumi also, accompanied by her father and her daughters, comes to her parental house. If others submit themselves to introspection and rumination to regain confidence, Sumi straightaway decides to face the facts squarely. Almost after 23 years of her marriage with Gopal, a history lecturer in a local college, one evening, for reasons even he cannot articulate, in a very casual way walks out and unburdens his responsibilities as husband and as a father of three grown up children. Even before Sumi realises the enormity of the situation and burden thrust on her, everything ends leaving, Sumi in a shocked silence. Though deserted by her husband for no fault of hers, Sumi learns to pick up the threads of her life. If Sumi is nonchalant at

Gopal's exit, Premi, Sumi's sister reacts violently. She is filled with anger because of the carelessness shown by both Sumi and Gopal towards their lives. There does not appear any obvious reason for Gopal's walking out of his family. His inward thoughts always remain unsaid to anybody. Unlike any other in her place, Sumi does not seek any explanation from Gopal though it is she who bears all the disgrace and humiliation. She surrounds herself with a death-like silence which can convey her pain more effectively than words can express. In a conversation Shashi Deshpande says to Vimala Rama Rao, "The reality dawns upon her without even any exchange of words. And Sumi understands and accepts it. Sumi's acceptance is not passive. She blocks out the unpleasantness. She has a good opinion of herself; she is more concerned with getting on with life. She does not want pity; she would do anything for pride. She distances even her husband. The point is, they are both unusual."[13] Revealing an independent and individualistic spirit just as her predecessors Indu, Saru, Jaya and Urmi have done, Sumi refuses to accept any kind of economic assistance either from her parents or from Premi, her doctor sister or from Ramesh, Gopal's doctor nephew. Working as a teacher, though on a temporary basis, she wants to stand on her own legs and assess her identity. As Sumi picks up her heart and prepares for the future, she thinks, "....... retracing my steps, picking up things, thinking – is this it? But she has turned resolutely away from even her immediate past, she is preparing herself for the future...."[14] She looks for a permanent Job, and with great determination learns to ride a two-wheeler, at her age. As soon as she learns to balance her drive, she throws up her arms in triumph of her success. She even decides to move out of her parent's house to live independently with her daughters and frantically searches for a house. Though her parents do not consider them as a burden, Sumi is unwilling to stay there. Later, however, she is persuaded to give up the idea considering the impracticalities associated with moving out of the big house, which is spacious enough to accommodate her family, into an expensive and congested apartment. Till Sumi picks up the threads of her life and shows her will-power and independence, she appears to be a spineless woman and an indifferent moron, too dull to grasp the situation. Though beautiful, educated and courageous, she lacks the spark of Indu, Saru, Jaya and Urmi. At the age of forty, Sumi starts her life afresh. But Sumi's daughter Aru is a rebel. She revolts against her father. She approaches Gopal not expecting sympathy for her or for her mother. She wants to unravel the strange behaviour of her father. She asks her father "why did you get married at all, why did you have children?" (MT, 65) Her searching question makes him re-examine his motives in fleeing from the family Aru is most affected by this event. She becomes aware of the neighbour's eyes following her family's movement. Aru resents the fact that their family appears so pathetic and vulnerable. She is also disappointed to see the tragedy of her grandmother and mother. Out of frustration, she declares that she is never going to get married. She holds strong views on patriarchy and how women in general, get victimised as a result of the actions of men. She is critical of Gopal. She wants to see that Gopal does not go Scot free. She also wants Sumi to file a case against Gopal. Shashi Deshpande flashes some light on the cause of women's education and liberation. Then the whole novel is devoted to silent, brooding women, unhappy, yet lively, clinging to their past, yet living in the present. This novel is infact an exploration of a woman's inner life. Through the character of Aru, the novelist looks hopefully at the younger generation to penetrate the silence, make women realise their situation and speak up for them. Inheriting her mother's pride and dignity courage and confidence, Aru assures her father that they will be all right: "We'll be quite alright, don't worry about us." (MT, 246) She says. modern and liberal in outlook, Sumi defies the outdated social opinion and orthodox treatment of a woman subjected to desertion by her husband. She has the courage to rise above the consequential problems and difficulties, humiliations, and frustrations. She has the generosity to gracefully free her husband from marital bonds without venting Ill-feelings. Sumi thus comes a long way from Indu, Jaya Saru and even Urmi for whom marriage is mostly the be-all and end-all of their existence. They dread seclusion and disintegration resulting from a broken marriage and hence opt for a compromise without of course losing their individualities. But Sumi is confident of her capabilities to make choices and assumes control over her life. The courage, the dignity, the responsibility, and the independent spirit displayed by her proves that she has reached a stage of self-sufficiency and self-fulfillment. She proves that women like her are capable of ushering in a positive change in the social structure.

The issues and themes in the novels of Shashi Deshpande, arise from the situation of women at the crossroads of transitional society, changing from traditional to modern. In *Small Remedies*, the novelist analyses the characters against the cultural modes and values that have given Indian women their image and role in society while probing the Indian woman's identity and her quest for space and selfhood. *Small Remedies* is a woman centered novel where Shashi Deshpande describes the period of about a year in the life of Madhu, the narrator of the story. Madhu seems to be sinking in grief, feels urged to seek a space for herself, to establish her own identity and worth as a woman. A series of grief-causing incidents are narrated or recalled from memory in the novel to show how these have been compressed in the unconscious plane of Madhu's character. The past also intrudes into the present, causing havoc in Madhu's married life. Shashi Deshpande explores the repercussions of these events and the feelings of grief, guilt and remorse that overwhelm the character. The novel clearly bears the stamp of Shashi Deshpande's writing. In the manner typical to her writing the story is revealed through the inner consciousness of one central character; life around is focused through the eyes of this character and understood through the mind of this one character. Not just in this aspect but also in her special way of looking at details, love for imagery, in her deliberately slow manner of unveiling the plot that is full of sudden twists and turns, in her ability to look into the depths of human heart and give expression to the feelings buried in there, and in the very honesty with which her central character confronts her own life, in the importance given to dreams to unravel events. *Small Remedies* is about the creative process, more so than any of her other novels. Madhu has written one biography and is in the process of writing another and as she collects her facts, works on the details, she looks closely at both the material and the process. She has enough material, but is it enough? It is easy enough to place it in a sequential order without worrying about the gaps. But that is not the way life is lived, and that is not the way its act is put together. What was required was the hidden truth beneath the hard reality. The felt emotions, the thwarted dreams, the selves destroyed, all of them need to be taken into account. In Bai's case, there are other problems. Besides the truth she has always struggled to hide, there is the fact that her life cannot be treated as raw material to be handled in the way one wants. Her life cannot be appropriated, it cannot be imagined as unreal; neither can she be allowed to get away with half-truth. Madhu examines her own role as a writer. When Madhu accepts the job of writing the life of Savitribai, Som is glad that she is going away for a while, and he is to be left alone to sort out his own confused state. Like Madhu, who is suffocated by grief, Som also feels the need to be himself, to recover his balance, to cope with the conflicting emotions that refuse to calm down. At the moment he cannot face his wife and longs to be apart, to be alone. He, too, needs space, and room to think, to be himself. For Madhu, it is an attempt to emancipate herself from her grief. Madhu's tangled emotions and feelings are arranged and rearranged within her until her perspective of life becomes clear. When Madhu separates temporarily from Som, it is to seek a female space where she can be comfortable with herself, where she can be the person she wants to be, self-accepted and self-actualised. In the late part of the novel, when Madhu arrives in Bhavanipur and prepares to begin a new life, playing the role of writer, she begins the process of recovery from her grief. In the home of Hari and Lata, she is given a room to call her very own, where she can be alone, free, and undisturbed. She is now capable of new thoughts and new ideas as the writer of Savitribai's biography. As the days pass, the inner turmoil, anger, and humiliation at her husband's rejection are all rearranged in the inner landscape of her mind and Madhu moves towards reconciliation to her grief and, to her husband also. Hence in *Small Remedies,* the novelist analyses the protagonist's conflicting thoughts on her husband's rejection and misunderstanding. At the same time Shashi Deshpande describes the suffering, distress, and seclusion that Madhu undergoes before she is reconciled to her grief and once again establishes a place for herself in society as Som's wife and, above all, as a human being. In the novel Shashi Deshpande shows her concern for the lot of women in Indian society and her writing is inseparable for the milieu she describes and the reader for whom she writes. The novel shows that there are many different problems in a woman's personal and family life. The novelist has skillfully voiced her fears and concerns regarding the future of women who, like Madhu, are being misunderstood and pass-through great turmoil and suffering in their quest for space and selfhood. Shashi Deshpande makes an aesthetic plea to free woman from the traditional male domination. The protagonist in *Small Remedies,* successfully breaks free of the stereotypes that bind her and arrives at a way of defining herself. It is also a novel that clearly marks the development of the personal philosophy of the writer. It tells us that there is no such homage that can protect us, that there is really no protection from life's disasters. All that we can hope for are remedies, and for these we do not have to look beyond the little acts of kindness that people around us extend to us.

In the novels of Shashi Deshpande, the respect for tradition, veneration of elders and responsibilities towards the family are still some of the most cherished values. The dichotomy between these traditional values and the urge towards individual self-fulfillment that marks modernity can often lead to a clash. Rejection of these values will take away something of great human worth from our social system, but an uncritical prolongation can lead to a suffocation of an individual's sense of self. For the new woman learning to think for herself yet firmly attached to many traditional values and attitudes, the way out often lies in a conscious, voluntary accommodation and adjustment. Saru in *The Dark Holds No Terrors*, and Indu in *Roots and Shadows* are, on the surface, successful emancipated women with fulfilling careers; Shashi Deshpande shows that in reality, they have not yet emotionally extricated themselves from patriarchal impositions, both direct and indirect. Obsessed as she is by the role of ideal home maker and self-sacrificing wife, Shashi Deshpande's woman has yet attempted to find her own voice. As a writer, the novelist has made depiction of the forces-external, and internal-conditioning the whole process of women's writing. Deeply concerned with problems that agitate women, Shashi Deshpande presents case studies in which protagonists probe their own selves to find how wrong had been their assessment of the self and how stupid and silly martyrs, they had been by refusing to become normal. Having lived long in tension, having despised many, and having wronged almost every member of the family, they discover that hatred, jealousy, or antagonism lead one nowhere. In the process of introspection and antagonism Shashi Deshpande's protagonists fail to come to terms with reality and are maladjusted whereas most of the males are well adjusted. It is not that the males escape bruises or humiliation, but they have a capacity to push their humiliation to deeper recesses of unconscious and manage to keep them tightly suppressed. They do not parade their bruises. The disgust of living with a man who does not love the woman the way she expects him to do is a burning problem that educated women face in our contemporary society. The novelist has portrayed the inner struggle of an artist to express herself, to discover her real self through her inner and instinctive potential for creative writing. Shashi Deshpande is not unconcerned about Indian reality in respect of the lot of women, but she is not a strident and militant kind of feminist who sees the male as the sole cause of woman's problems.

In her earlier as well as later novels, it is not the aim of Shashi Deshpande to merely document female resistance to patriarchal ideologies, but also to focus on the strategies and readjustments her female protagonists undertake in order to forge an identity of their own. Her women characters struggle to learn to become 'one's own refuge' and value the fellowships of other women. She recreates sensitively the female world through modes of women's experience and links it to the larger world of human existence and by doing so she gives it the mainstream position. She refuses to seclude women's experience even as her fiction consciously creates feminine sensibility and specificity and is at times even successful in creating a language of her own. The movement of the Shashi Deshpande woman character from her parental home to the outside world, through education and marriage, does not really initiate her into knowledge of the self. Their defiance of the mother does not ensure them the freedom they desire. Their return home, in the absence of the mother only helps them realise their own selves. They had imagined that their mothers stifled their growth and so defied them. But when husbands begin to kill the very roots of their existence, they defied their husbands and find a way of their own, rejecting all over-ridding influences. Their fear of losing themselves in the dark mysterious universe is dispelled by their understanding that one can believe in one's self and accept the responsibility for one's life.

## Notes And References

1. Anuradha Roy. "Patterns of Feminist Consciousness" In *Indian Women Writers: A Study of Anita Desai's Cry, the Peacock, Nayantara Sahgal's Storm in Chandigarh,* Attia Hosain's Sunlight on A Broken Column, Rama Mehta's Inside the Haveli and Shashi Deshpande's That Long Silence, (New Delhi: Prestige Books, 1999), 70, hereafter cited in the chapter.
2. Sukrita Paul Kumar. "Decoding Gender in Literary Texts", *Indian Literature,* 1993, 157.
3. Dr. N. Sethuraman. "Silence, Surrender and Compromise? A Study of Shashi Deshpande's That Long Silence", ed. by. K. Balachandran, *Critical Responses to Indian Writing in English: Essays in Honour of Dr. A.P.J.* Abdul Kalam. (New Delhi: Sarup & Sons, 2004), 165.
4. N.B. Masal. "Shashi Deshpande's A Matter of Time: As an Exploration of a Woman's Inner Life", ed. by, T.M.J. Indra Mohan, *Shashi Deshpande: A Critical Spectrum,* (New Delhi: Atlantic Publishers & Distributors, 2004), 146.

5. Prasanna Sree Sathupati. "Conflict and Identity in Shashi Deshpande's Novels", *Indian Women Novelists*: Set III: Vol.4, ed. by. R.K. Dhawan, (New Delhi: Prestige Books, 1995), 17.
6. Shashi Deshpande. *The Dark Holds No Terrors*, (New Delhi: Penguin Books, 1990), 37, here after cited in the chapter.
7. Sarla Palkar. "Breaking The Silence: That Long Silence", *Indian Women Novelists* Set I. Vol: V, ed. by. R.K. Dhawan, (New Delhi: Prestige Books, 1991), 169.
8. Shashi Deshpande. *That Long Silence*, (London: Virgo Press, 1988), 7, here after cited in the chapter.
9. Shashi Deshpande. *Roots and Shadows*, (Hyderabad: Disha Books, 1992), 34, here after cited in the chapter.
10. O.P. Bhatnagar. *Indian Womanhood: Fight for Freedom in Shashi Deshpande's Roots And Shadows*, 45.
11. Indira Nityanandam. "Shashi Deshpande's The Binding Vine: Silent No More", *Indian Woman Novelists*, Set. III, Vol.4, 66.
12. Vimala Rama Rao. "A Well-Articulated Silence". Rev. of That Long Silence, *The Literary Criterion*, Vol.27, No.4, 1992, 76-77.
13. Shashi Deshpande. *A Matter of Time,* (New Delhi, Penguin books, 1996), 65, here after cited in the chapter.

# CHAPTER 6

# Conclusion

In the forgoing chapters of this thesis, an attempt has been made to raise important issues and questions relating to the dilemma of seclusion, search for identity and affirmation. On the basis of the analyses of the writings of Shashi Deshpande, particularly her novels, and getting motivation from the studies of Indian scholars, the forbidding task of searching and finding appropriate answers relating specifically to the questions arising out of the wide-ranging perception and concern of the prominent novelist, has been undertaken sitting at the lotus feet of goddess Saraswati. The findings that thus emerged are incorporated in different forms in accordance with the focus enjoined upon the study by a suitable emphasis in every chapter. The preceding chapters have been devoted to the study of women protagonists in the novels of Shashi Deshpande. She portrays modern, educated and career oriented middle class married woman who is sensitive to the changing times and situations. Revealing a remarkable insight into the nature of a woman's mind, she depicts woman in myriad roles – wife, mother, daughter, and an individual in her own right. She always concerns herself with a woman's search for her identity. She endeavours to establish woman as an individual who breaks loose from the traditional constraints and refines her identity in tune with the changed social ambience of the modern times.

The first chapter has taken note of the conceptual framework of the literary, philosophical, and psychological aspects of the concept of feminism in the context of the perplexities and paradoxes, dilemma and predicaments faced by the woman. A clear picture of this concept emerges from the views of writers, scholars, social reformers, and theoreticians such as Simone de Beauvoir, Betty Friedan, Kate Millett, Elaine Showalter, Germaine Greer, Sylvia Plath, Margaret Drabble, Doris Lessing, Iris Murdoch, Marilyn French, Margaret Atwood, Jane Austen, Emily Bronte, Stevie Smith,

Charlotte Mew, Mananne Moor, and Elizabeth Bishop. Indian scholars and writers such as Raja Rao, R.K. Narayan, Mulk Raj Anand, Rabindranath Tagore and also women novelists such as Santha Rama Rau, Kamala Markandaya, Ruth Prawer Jhabvala, Nayantara Sahgal, Anita Desai, Shobha de, Manju Kapur and Arundhati Roy have also tried to define this literary term in Indian context. *The Making of the Novelist* has given the required information about the novelist. Her family aura, education, social values, surroundings, circumstances, philosophy, works and furthermore her own experiences and influences play a very crucial role in making her a novelist. A close study of Shashi Deshpande's novels reveals her enormous sympathy for woman and her travails, provoking reviewers to assume that she has joined the group of feminist writers who have achieved much popularity in the west. She, however, does not approve of being labelled a feminist writer. Though Shashi Deshpande refuses to be called a feminist writer, her novels are susceptible to a feminist approach. She has a remarkable insight into the working of a woman's mind. As a writer, she highlights the secondary position occupied by women and their degradation which is inevitable in an oppressively male dominated society. She gives us a peep into the state and condition of the present-day woman who is intelligent and articulate, aware of her capabilities, but thwarted under the weight of male chauvinism. Shashi Deshpande's women are the products of a painful period of transition in society where they have a greater share of responsibilities than their predecessors. They also have a number of avenues open before them and in many fields; they have also proved themselves better than their male counterparts. In spite of their remarkable achievements, the general attitude towards women has not changed correspondingly. In the institution of marriage, the age-old rules with regard to the accepted behaviour of husband and wife remain almost unchanged, despite an overt display of western influence. Shashi Deshpande's novels are concerned with a woman's search for her identity, an exploration into the female psyche. Her protagonists undergo an arduous journey to discover themselves and this leads them through a maze of self-doubts and fears. According to Suvarna Shinde, "Shashi Deshpande's novels depict the anguish, agony, and conflict of the modern, educated Indian women caught between patriarchy and tradition on the one hand and self-expression, individuality and independence on the other."[1] In her novels, she depicts woman in myriad roles – wife, mother, daughter, and an individual in her own right.

The second chapter has been devoted to study and analyse the dilemma of a woman who carries the burden of her own overblown ego right from her early childhood. Whether she is reared as an ignored sibling or as a pampered child, she grows with complexes overconscious of her superiority. It there is a doting father who showers affection, there is, inevitably, an antagonism with mother. Shashi Deshpande examines this problem like a naturalist. She keeps on separating the threads of reality till she arrives at nothingness. She treads through the subconscious towards uncovering the unconscious in order to reach the truth. Her essential merit is shown in delineation of characters who are always individual who is pitted against social absurdities and overbearing nature. Here in she comes closer to the existential view of life. The mother had appeared an authority figure and posed a threat to her individuality and self-will. The mother in the novels of Shashi Deshpande is not given much importance. Besides generation gap, a gap in the mother-daughter relationship is also highlighted. As it is, generally mothers impose the same restrictions upon their daughters that were imposed upon them by their own mothers. They do not realise the fact that the traditional middle-class idea that a woman's only career should be her family is now rejected by the up coming girls who are very much influenced by factors such as the spread of scientific ideas, the growing impact of other cultures on the individuals, and the availability of a vast body of literature. Though most of the educated working women still give preference to marriage and their family life, which according to Shashi Deshpande should not be neglected, the wish to be economically independent, to have an individual identity in the society is more pronounced among the majority of women than was found earlier. This becomes the reason why the girls insist on continuing their studies even when they do not get any support from their family. Saru, in *The Dark Holds No Terrors*, hates her mother as she puts all sorts of restrictions on her freedom. Even at the time of taking admission into a medical college, Saru does not seek her mother's advice but asks her father only giving more respect to him. Jaya, in *That Long Silence,* is typical of many women in dealings with her father. Similarly, Indu in *Roots and Shadows,* whose mother died in giving birth to her, sees her father almost as a god. There is the dilemma of seclusion in filial and familial bonds which leads the woman towards the feeling of aloofness, despair pessimism, seclusion, and loss of self. So, she needs to go out of her inner struggle and search her own identity.

The third chapter deals, in detail, with the hollowness of man-woman relationship. The type of society that is presented in the novels is patriarchal and male dominant where the wives are afraid of their husbands and cannot converse freely and frankly about the children going out of trace. Shashi Deshpande, in her novels, has also tried to see and define what an Indian marriage is in the traditional sense of the term. Getting the daughters married is a sense of achievement for the parents. There are no emotions involved in bringing the two different entities together. In *Roots and Shadows,* Indu defines marriage as: "What was marriage after all, but two people brought together after cold-blooded bargaining to meet, mate and reproduce so that the generations might continue."[2] Marriage locates itself in romance, sexuality and social environment. In *That Long Silence,* Jaya looks at a married couple as "a pair of bullocks yoked together."[3] Saru, in *The Dark Holds No Terrors,* marries a person who is not from her caste. Her mother predicts an unhappy married life: "You won't be happy with him. I know you won't. A man of a different caste, different community……what will you two have in common."[4] Marriage makes women dependent upon their husbands. Even economic independence does not assist them to get themselves disentangled from the emotional dependence and attachment. Lack of emotions and spiritual oneness between husband and wife is highlighted in the novels. Marriage cannot bring happiness to both the spouses unless they surrender their ego and merge into each other. But here we find that neither of the women protagonists is emotionally united with her husband as there is a difference in attitude towards life. In the novels under study, it is notable that the men characters are not very expressive. Perhaps Shashi Deshpande wanted to highlight the problems of women more than the unchanged attitude of the men folk. They keep silent about the issues, and, at the same time, they expect submissiveness from their spouses. Without mentioning and discussing the matters, they take it for granted that the women will follow them. For example, in *That Long Silence,* Mohan, Jaya's husband, takes it for granted that Jaya is going to follow his decision. When caught in malpractice, he makes his wife and children responsible for it that he cares for them so much that he went out of his way to get the things done: "I've always put you and the children first." (TLS, 12) Mohan explains to assure Jaya's company with him but he never looks into her demands and neither does she communicate anything directly to Mohan and hence there always remains a gap between husband and wife and silence prevails in the house. That is why marriage often becomes a prison for her protagonist; Urmi in *The Binding Vine,* does not reject it but tries to create more breathing space for herself as well as for other women within the structures of marriage and family. As Kamini Dinesh observes, "The wife, in the end, is therefore not a rebel but a redeemed wife – one who has broken the long silence, one who is no longer afraid of the dark. She is a wife reconceptualised as woman and an individual……"[5] Just as in Shashi Deshpande's novels one finds the critique of the patriarchal ideology which ignores women's aspirations for individuality beyond the confines of home and family, one also finds a rebuttal of the feminist ideology that does not seem to take cognisance of the great divide within women – their need for love and relationship. The basic point which the entire three women protagonists share, needs to be highlighted: they all are ultimately appendages to men. Due to their emotional pull towards the traditions in the beginning, they question the social mores, yet, they finally try their best to conform to their roles.

The fourth chapter takes cognisance of the fact that the identity crisis of the protagonists exhibited through the patterns of isolation produces secluded selves. Parent-child relationship is often like undercurrents, unrealised or unidentified, not really fully specified and often instrumental in fostering the dilemma of seclusion and inner conflicts until some hitherto unknown fact comes to light and a crisis takes place, which breaks down the barriers. Mother-daughter relationships in Shashi Deshpande's novels are at loggerheads but still mother is the most important relation in their lives. Motherhood has periodically been an obtrusive concern of woman in her novels. There is seclusion, silence, isolation, and lack of communication in parent-child relationship that makes the relationship unbearable. Mothers in the novels of Shashi Deshpande are secluded figure, working with in their limited preview with complete dominance by men and harassment by in-laws along with misunderstanding by daughters. Mother-child is not a one-to-one relationship. It is governed and shaped by the male presence, the husband, or the son, in its finer nuances. The halo around motherhood is clearly missing in Shashi Deshpande's novels.

Chapter five endows a new dimension to the whole phenomenon of seclusion. Infact, seclusion and affirmation are the two sides of the same coin; both are fundamental facts, of the human condition. If it is the process of seclusion with the help of which the important problem of identity or the identity crisis is analysed, elucidated, or contextualised, it is the process of affirmation that characterises the resolution of dilemmas and predicaments, to the extent possible with reference to the specificities of a situation. Shashi Deshpande's protagonists raise their voice against the straight-jacketed role models of daughter, sister, wife and mother and refuse to be the objects of cultural and social oppressions of age-old patriarchal society. The narration, in all the novels, shifts from present to the past covering the whole life span of the protagonists. All the time they are brooding over their fate, questioning them what they really are and ultimately trying to adapt themselves to the surroundings. Her women protagonists revolt against social taboos, the cramped, wrinkled traditions and values of their ancestors and ceaselessly question the very concepts of love, marriage, and sex, and feel and urge to redefine human relationship and behaviour. The novels end with an optimistic note with the hope of some positive action in the future. For example, Saru in *The Dark Holds No Terrors,* waits for her husband to come to take her back and start their life afresh, Indu in *Roots and Shadows,* plans to go back to her husband and tell him everything about herself, and Jaya in *That Long Silence,* interprets Mohan's letter in positive terms and hopes for the better.

The struggle of women in Shashi Deshpande's novels is to give shape and content to their individual existence in society, culminates in a crisis and ends in compromise. New bonds replace the old; that's all. In the end comes the realisation that freedom lies in having the courage to do what one believes is the right thing to do and the determination and the tenacity to it. That alone can bring harmony in life. Thus, perhaps the writer has tried to convey to the society that the need of the time, in this transitional phase, is not a total revolt but a gradual change in the society for which everyone has to put some effort to bridge the gap between the old and the new generation.

Shashi Deshpande's novels are all about growing up – not through an adolescent period but growing up into selfhood – once the characters are able to outgrow, the traditional training imparted to a girl child and the socialisation which renders her docile and obedient. Indu in *Roots and Shadows,* has been married for three years, Saru in *The Dark Holds No Terrors,* nearly fifteen and Sumi in *A Matter of Time,* too has three teenaged daughters when her twenty-odd year marriage collapses and Madhu in *Small Remedies,* has just lost a seventeen year old son. Married women of the world in some ways, they have yet to find their way in the world, to move through the process of separation towards a concept of the self. Except for *Roots and Shadows,* where the crisis is not self-related, the other novels begin with a crisis in the lives of the women protagonists. Jaya is shaken out of her notion of respectability and huddled into semi-hiding in the Dadar-flat. Saru moves from rejection of her parental home to the rejection of her marital home, Sumi is thrown out of her wifely role in one stroke, and Madhu is bereaved and experiences a sense of both abandonment and loss. They are up against forces that they do not fully comprehend. Urmi has also undergone bereavement, but the focus is not so much on Urmi as on Mira and Kalpana in *The Binding Vine,* where the body is pinned down against the woman's wish, curbing her freedom. The imposition of physical relationship on them is contrasted with its absence in Urmi's case, where Kishore is away for long stretches. These women have to work through their sense of sustenance. *The Binding Vine* is a refreshing change from the earlier novels of Shashi Deshpande. According to Indira Nityanandam: "The step forward, achieved in this novel, is the introduction of female bonding, the desire of one woman to help another less fortunate one. Urmila draws society's attention to the plight of the rape victim and is determined to get Mira's poems published. This is a positive development in the protagonist, for Sarita, Jaya and Indu were involved in fighting only their own battles."[6] Families may disperse in *Roots and Shadows,* economic security threatened in *That Long Silence,* bodily freedom assaulted in *The Dark Holds No Terrors,* and apparently happy marriages collapse in *A Matter of Time*. What happens then? How and where does a woman find means of self-sustenance, growth, and life? The other man wherever he is – Naren in *Roots and Shadows,* Kamat in *That Long Silence,* Padmakar in *The Dark Holds No Terrors,* Bhaskar in *The Binding Vine,* is either dead or discarded. Male support is not fully accepted. In *A Matter of Time,* Sumi is reluctant to go on staying with Vishwas and is equally reluctant to accept Ramesh's help, and in *Small Remedies,* Madhu finds herself looked upon with suspicion when she spends the night in a hotel. Women have, over centuries, been treated as exchange items between men – from father to husband, and at times, as in Kalpana's case, to an uncle who wants to take her as a second wife. The female self, in order to emerge in its own right, has first to validate her existence on her own terms, without male protection or support. A woman does not necessarily or automatically grow into a self. She has to acquire her identity. In Sumi's case, this idea comes to its realisation in a sense it does not happen with either Jaya or Indu. She begins to accept the idea of exploring freedom and living for herself. Saru, too, finds a new source of sustenance in her profession. It is no longer merely a source of income or self-assurance, but her very being as she nurses Madhav and attends to the neighbour's child. Nirmala Prakash observes: "Shashi Deshpande's novels despite all the suffering, tension and agony that her protagonists undergo, end on an optimistic note."[7] Shashi Deshpande's novels are concerned with a woman's search for her identity. Her protagonists undergo an arduous journey to discover themselves and this leads them through a maze of self-doubts and fears. Shashi Deshpande, as a feminist, strongly resents the border-line position of women and feels it necessary to defend women as women in order to counteract the patriarchal oppression that precisely despises women as women. Shashi Deshpande does not take kindly to the theory that women are victims. The dependency syndrome in women is responsible for their victimisation and she desires that women need to offer resistance and emerge as strong-willed individuals to face life, to share responsibilities and not to escape from it.

The sensitivity and compassion with which Shashi Deshpande approaches her characters, is clear from the fact that in order to reveal the beauty and ugliness of life, she employs characters having acute sensitivity to its grandeur as well as sordidness. She is not a visionary or a mystic, but an artist who shows the sorrow underlying the grandest things, and the grandeur underlying the sorriest things. The basic problem shown in her novels is how to exist in society, and yet maintain one's individuality.

In all Shashi Deshpande's novels except *Come Up and Be Dead*, the protagonists are married women. Hence her depiction of woman as wife requires special mention. According to Rani Dharkar, "the importance that our society attaches to marriage is reflected in our literature. It is the central concern of Shashi Deshpande whose heroines, caught in the quagmire of marriage, struggle to come up for air."[8] Marriage is, perhaps, the most complex of human relationships. Shashi Deshpande presents the inequalities and injustice heaped on woman because of her subordinate status. In *Roots and Shadows,* through the eyes of Indu, the protagonist, we are made aware of the plight of various women like her Kakis and Atyas. The heart-rending account of Akka's child marriage reveals the appalling condition of women barely a couple of generations ago. The inferior position of a wife in any marriage is made obvious through glimpses into the marriages of Indu's numerous aunts and uncles. It is clear that Indu, who is proud of her liberated outlook, appears as a prey to age-old tradition and unreasonable convention. She is one who, in her quest to be independent realises that there is beauty and security in life through reconciliation. Indu's predicament is representative of the larger predicament of women in general in contemporary Indian society which is passing through a transition from the old cultural modes to the new social and economic forces impinging effectively on the pattern of human lives. Indu represents a woman torn between age-old traditions and individual views. Because of her awareness of the sanctity of the familial bonds, she restrains herself from the precipitous action of fleeing from the domestic scene. Though she views these bonds as unreasonable in the beginning, gradually, she learns to be bound by them as a typical traditional Indian woman, for she knows that transgressing them will certainly rupture the family ties. She realises that it would be wise to seek freedom without undermining her obligations and responsibilities and without losing her individuality. Indu's decision not to submit herself to anyone's dictates, not to get influenced by her husband in career matters shows that she is making independent decisions. Her search for freedom results in her emergence as a bold and challenging woman of determination. She negates all feminine limitations and also acquires the power to change others.

Saru's husband, Manohar in *The Dark Holds No Terrors,* is a glaring example of men with fragile egos, who find it difficult to accept the superior status of their wives in society. Shashi Deshpande also holds society responsible for the disastrous condition of Saru's marriage, Manu, who already suffers from an inferiority complex, is further humiliated by the cruel remarks of his colleague's wife and those of the girl who interviews Saru. The title *The Dark Holds No Terrors,* is self-explanatory. The irony involved is far from being abstract. Darkness implies incapability to see things clearly and objectively. Darkness is a source of constant fear from outside. It affects the outlook of the inside, but it holds no terror in itself. Saru is the representative of middle-class working women in modern India, rebelling against traditions but ultimately trying to compromise with existing reality. When her professional success has cast a shadow on her married life, she undergoes a trauma, but eventually stands up to the situation. She realises that escapism is never a solution and that she is her own refuge. She succeeds in realising her selfhood through her profession and proves to the world that economically independent women like her can bring change in the society and that woman as individuals can have some significant control over their relationships and professions. Her promise of reconciliation with her husband is not her defeat or submission but her newfound confidence to confront reality. Thus, she achieves freedom and harmony in life without compromising on her obligations and responsibilities.

In *That Long Silence,* Shashi Deshpande has woven the tragic tales of Jaya's relations and her acquaintances into the texture of the novel. Due to her sensitive nature, Jaya is very particular about moulding her tastes in order to suit those of the rest even if her superior intellect is not satisfied. In the very beginning of the novel, we see that she tries to reason-out with her father as to why she should not listen to the songs broadcast on the radio, but ultimately, she keeps silent, suppressing her desire. Here, Shashi Deshpande has presented the theme of lack of communication. As she herself declares: "The themes of lack of communication may be over-familiar in western fiction, but in extrovert India it is not much analysed."[9] Jaya is basically a modern woman rooted in tradition, whereas her husband, Mohan, is a traditionalist rooted in customs. The difference between their outlooks is so great that they fail, time and again, to understand each other. The difference in their attitude is the main cause of their failure to understand each other. In her stream of thoughts, Jaya, too, looks at her marital relations where there is no conversation left between them. She realises that in order to attain self-hood, a woman must transcend silence, negation, and seclusion. A woman's relation with her family must burgeon within the totality of her life as a woman. Her decision to cease to be a passive partner and overcome the turbulence in her relationship with Mohan leads her to an uninhibited self-identification. The novel clearly spells out the faith that a woman's desire to succeed like an individual does not negate or cancel her desire for love, marriage, and domesticity. A balanced and purposeful life is not a utopian fancy for a woman if she liberates herself from the stereotyped conditioning of society and is not dependent on the male presence to authenticate her thoughts, emotions, and deeds at every step. In the novel, Shashi Deshpande has presented not a woman who revolts openly in the beginning and later on reconciles to the situation, but a kind of woman who wants to revolt, but ultimately does not. Her inner turmoil is so bitter that she is unable to speak them out and remains silent in order not to be frustrated and disappointed after the disapproval of her actions by the society. According to Sarabjit Sandhu: "Jaya is unable to unfold the truth. Her image becomes like that of a bird who has got wings and knows that it can fly, but, somehow, does not. In the same way, Jaya is aware of her abilities, and she knows that she can expose them openly, but somehow, she does not."[10]

In *The Binding Vine*, Shashi Deshpande raises the issue of hitherto untouched issue of marital rape. Women like Mira, Urmi's mother-in-law have to bear the nightly physical assault by their husbands silently. Other women like Shakutai, her sister Sulu, Kalpana and her sister have their own sorry tales. Shakutai's husband is a drunkard and a good-for-nothing fellow, who leaves his wife and children for another woman. Kalpana is brutally raped by Prabhakar, Sulu's husband. Urmi takes up cudgels on Kalpana's behalf and the culprit is caught. On the other hand, is Urmi. Her husband is in navy and during his long absence she craves for some physical gratification. Her friendship with Dr. Bhaskar provides her ample opportunity, but she never oversteps the boundaries chalked out in marriage. But the painful aspect to this is that this virtue of hers will remain unacknowledged by her husband. *The Binding Vine*, has its beginning in a personal loss – the death of Urmi's daughter Anu. Urmi's loss is of a different kind than that of Saru or Indu. They had lost a mother or a mother surrogate from whom they had already been separated. Their personal dilemmas were more urgent to them than these bereavements. Like most of the protagonists of Shashi Deshpande, Urmila is not dependent upon men for survival and asserts both her economic as well as psychological independence. She is the voice of resistance in the novel which registers a protest against the patriarchal attitude to the issue of rape.

*A Matter of Time,* is yet another novel where in the husband walks out on his family comprising the wife and three daughters. Sumi, the protagonist, is so shocked that she lapses into complete silence but, apparently tries hard to keep things normal for her daughters. Her desertion is a cause for great humiliation and mental trauma for her as it is not only a matter of great shame and disgrace but a bitter realisation of being unwanted. Words of sympathy from relations fail to console her. At the age of forty, deserted by her husband, she stands alone and helpless along with three teenaged daughters. But she is not emotionally shattered as is common with housewives without economic independence. On the other hand, she demonstrates strength and maturity even in adversity. She displays rare courage and self-confidence in trying to cope with the consequential problems and difficulties, humiliations, and frustrations, all by her. Unlike any other in her place, she has the generosity to gracefully free her husband from marital bonds without venting ill-feelings. Her desertion, instead of making her an emotional wreck, has surprisingly brought out the real, hidden strength in her. She desires to be economically independent and asserts her identity. She revives even her creativity. She, thus, comes a long way from Indu, Jaya, Saru and even Urmi for whom marriage is mostly the be-all and end-all of their existence. The courage, the dignity, the responsibility, and the independent spirit displayed by her proves that she has reached a stage of self-sufficiency and self-fulfillment.

Shashi Deshpande explores in *If I Die Today*, her favourite themes, of which woman's condition remains her principal preoccupation. The novelist examines the plight of women from a different perspective by presenting the case of an economically independent non-Hindu family and there by suggesting that the fate of woman remains the same irrespective of caste, culture, religion or economic status.

Another novel *Small Remedies,* clearly bears the stamp of Shashi Deshpande's writing. In the manner typical to her writing the story is revealed through the inner consciousness of one central character; life around is focused through the eyes of this character and understood through the mind of this one character. Not just in this aspect but also in her special way of looking at details, love for imagery, in her deliberately slow manner of unveiling the plot that is full of sudden twists and turns, in her ability to look into the depths of human heart and give expression to the feelings buried in there, and in the very honesty with which her central character confronts her own life, in the importance given to dreams to unravel events, this is a Shashi Deshpande, book.

*Moving On,* Shashi Deshpande's latest novel, explores the private lives of women, while situating these private lives in public contexts. The novelist does not envisage this female bonding as a solution to male domination, but she is confident that it is certainly a comfort to the oppressed women. Shashi Deshpande appears to believe that by not protesting and offering resistance, the women have to blame themselves for their own victimisation. She, therefore, suggests that they themselves have to break the shackles that have kept them in a state of captivity for several centuries. Thus, the novelist has tried to convey to the society that the need of the time, in this transitional phase, is not a total revolt but a gradual change in the society by which everyone has to put some effort to bridge the gap between the old and the new generation.

Shashi Deshpande's protagonists finally try their best to conform to their roles, and the novels end with an optimistic note with the possibility of some positive action in future. With this study, all the dilemmas, obstacles, conflicts and struggles in the lives of woman, in the novels of Shashi Deshpande, are explicit. Due to these problems, there is a loneliness and seclusion in the mind and heart of woman.

## Notes And References


1. Suvarna Shinde. "Quest For Freedom: A Study of Margaret Laurence's, *A Jest of God,* and Shashi Deshpande's *A Matter Of Time,* ed. by, Suman Bala. *Woman in the Novels of Shashi Deshpande,* (New Delhi: Khosla Publishing House, 2001), 127.
2. Shashi Deshpande. *Roots And Shadows,* (Hyderabad: Disha Books, 1992), 3, here after cited in the chapter.
3. Shashi Deshpande. *That Long Silence,* (London: Virgo Press, 1988), 3, here after cited in the chapter.
4. Shashi Deshpande. *The Dark Holds No Terrors,* (New Delhi: Penguin Books, 1990), 90, here after cited in the chapter.
5. Kamini Dinesh. "Moving Out of The Cloistered Self: Shashi Deshpande's Protagonists", ed. by, Jasbir Jain & Amina Amin. *Margins of Erasure: Purdah in the Subcontinental Novel in English,* (New Delhi: sterling Publishers private limited, 1995, 1995), 20.
6. Indira Nityanandam. "Shashi Deshpande's The Binding Vine: Silent No More," *Indian Woman Novelists* Set III, Vol.-4, 66.

7. Nirmala Prakash. "From Margin to the Centre: Shashi Deshpande and Arundhati Roy", ed. by. T.M.J. Indra Mohan, *Shashi Deshpande: A Critical Spectrum,* (New Delhi: Atlantic Publishers & Distributors, 2004), 204.
8. Rani Dharker. "Marriage As Purdah: Fictional Rendering of a Social Reality," *Margins of Erasure: Purdah in the Sub-Continental Novel in English*, ed. Jasbir Jain and Amina Amin, (New Delhi: Sterling, 1995), 50.
9. Interview with Shashi Deshpande by John Cunningham. "Indian Writer's Block", *The Indian Post,* March-6, 1988.
10. Sarabjit Sandhu. *The Image of Woman in That Long Silence,* (New Delhi: Prestige Books, 1991), 36-44.

# Bibliography


## 1. Primary Sources

### *Novels*

Deshpande, Shashi. *If I Die Today,* (New Delhi: Vikas Publishing House, 1982).

Deshpande, Shashi. *Come Up and Be Dead,* (New Delhi: Vikas Publishing House, 1983).

Deshpande, Shashi. *That Long Silence,* (London: Virgo Press, 1988).

Deshpande, Shashi. *The Dark Holds No Terrors,* (New Delhi: Penguin Books, 1990).

Deshpande, Shashi. *Roots And Shadows,* (Hyderabad: Disha books, 1992).

Deshpande, Shashi. *The Binding Vine,* (New Delhi: Penguin books 1993).

Deshpande, Shashi. *A Matter of Time,* (New Delhi: Penguin books 1996).

Deshpande, Shashi. *Small Remedies,* (New Delhi: Viking, Penguin 2000).

Deshpande, Shashi. *Moving On,* (New Delhi: Penguin books 2004).

### *Essays And Articles*

Deshpande, Shashi. *The Hindu,* online edition of India's National Newspaper. Monday, Feb 16, 2004.

Deshpande, Shashi. "Timeless Masterpiece." *Indian Review of Books.* Vol.4, No.1, Oct-Dec. 1994.

### *Interviews And Conversations*

"An Interview with Shashi Deshpande" by Aditi De. *Breaking That Long Silence,* May 7' 2002.

"An Interview with Shashi Deshpande" by Vanmala Viswanatha. A Woman's World ...... All The Way! *Literature Alive,* 1/3 December 1987.

"In Conversation with Shashi Deshpande" by Vimala Rama Rao, in R.S. Pathak's *The Fiction of Shashi Deshpande* (Creative Books, 1998).

## 2. Secondary Sources

### *Books On Shashi Deshpande*

Atrey, Mukta and Viney Kirpal. *Shashi Deshpande: A Feminist Study Of Her Fiction,* New Delhi: B.R. Publishing Corporation, 1998.

Bala, Suman. *Woman in the Novels of Shashi Deshpande,* New Delhi: Khosla Publishing House, 2001.

Iyenger, K.R. Srinivasa. *Indian Writing in English,* New Delhi: Sterling Publishers Private Limited, 2004.

Jain, Jasbir. *Gendered Realities, Human Spaces, the writing of Shashi Deshpande,* Jaipur: Rawat Publications 2003.

Mohan, T.M.J. Indra. *Shashi Deshpande: A Critical Spectrum,* New Delhi: Atlantic Publishers and Distributors, 2004.

Pathak, R.S. *The Fiction of Shashi Deshpande,* New Delhi: Creative Books, 1998.

Prasad, Amar Nath. *Indian Women Novelists in English,* New Delhi: Atlantic Publishers and Distributors, 2001.

Reddy, Y.S. Sunita. *A Feminist Perspective on The Novels of Shashi Deshpande,* New Delhi: Prestige Books, 2001.

Roy, Anuradha. *Patterns of Feminist Consciousness in Indian Women Writers: S A Study of Anita Desai's Cry, the Peacock, Nayantara Sahgal's Storm* In C Chandigarh, Attia Hosain's Sunlight On A Broken Column, Rama Mehta's Inside The Haveli and Shashi Deshpande's That Long Silence, New Delhi: Prestige Books, 1999.

Sandhu, Sarbjit K. *The image of woman in the Novels of Shashi Deshpande,* New Delhi: Prestige Books, 1991.

Sebastian, Mrinalini. *The Novels of Shashi Deshpande in Postcolonial Arguments,* New Delhi: Sangam Book, 2000.

Sharma, Siddhartha. *Shashi Deshpande's Novels: A Feminist Study,* New Delhi: Atlantic Publish and Distributors, 2005.

Sree, S. Prasanna. *Woman in the Novels of Shashi Deshpande: A Study.* New Delhi: Sarup & Sons, 2003.

### *Articles, Essays/Reviews*

Anandalakshmi, S. "The Female Child in A Family Setting", *The Indian Journal Of Social Work,* Vol. L II, No. 1, January 1991.

Awasthi, A.K. Shashi Deshpande's *'If I Die Today':* A Meistic Analysis", *Indian Fiction in English: Problems and Promises.* Pathak R. S. (Ed) New Delhi: Northern Book Centre, 1990.

Bande, Usha. *Mothers and Mother-Figures in Indo-English Literature.* Jalandhar: ABS Publications, 1994.

Baral, K.C. *Reading the mother: Psychoanalysis And Indian Novel Written In English,* ed. by. Usha Bande, Jalandhar: ABS Publications, 1994.

Barche, G.D. "Indu: Another Sisyphus in Shashi Deshpande's Roots and Shadows", *Creative Forum,* Vol.2, No. 3 & 4, Jul-Dec. 1989.

Basu, Tapan. "Joining A Select Club", *Review of That Long Silence,* Sunday, No. 8-14, May 1988, 98.

Bhatnagar, P. "Indian Womanhood: Fight for Freedom in Roots and Shadows", *Indian Women Novelists* Set I, Vol.V, ed. by. Dhawan, R.K, New Delhi: Prestige Books, 1991.

Bhatnagar, Parvati. "Search of Identity: A Study of Shashi Deshpande's The Dark Holds No Terror," *The Quest*, Vol.15, No.1, June 2001.

Bhatt, Indira. "That Long Silence: A Study", *Indian Women Novelists* Set I. Vol: V. Dhawan R.K. (Ed.) New Delhi: Prestige Books, 1991.

Desai, Anita. "Interview with Anita Desai", by. Yashodhara Dalmia, *The Times of India*, 29 April, 1979.

Dharkar, Rani. "Marriage as Purdah: Fictional Rendering of a Social Reality", *Margins of Erasure: Purdah in the Subcontinental Novel in English,* Jasbir Jain and Amina Amin (Ed.). New Delhi: Sterling Publishers, Private Limited, 1995.

Dickman, Sue. "In Conversation with Indian Women Writers", *The Book Review*, Vol. 19, No. 4, April, 1995.

Elaine Showalter, *A Literature of Their Own: British Women Novelists From Bronte To Lessing*; Princeton, NK: Princeton University Press, 1977.

Elizabeth Fox-Genovese, *Lexicon Universal Encyclopedia* Lexicon Publications, INC, New York. 1987,1985,1984,1983.

Gaur, Rashmi. "Images of Indian Woman in Shashi Deshpande's Long Silence Stereotypes, Myths and Realities". *The Literary Criterion*, Vol.38, No.1, 2003.

Gaur, Rashmi. "Suffering and Desire in Shashi Deshpande's Small Remedies". *The Quest,* Vol. 16, No. 1, June2002.

Gupta, Ramesh Kumar. "Images of Indian Woman in Shashi Deshpande's Novel Roots and Shadows: A Critical Study". *Poetcrit,* Vol.15, No.1, Jan, 2002.

Indira, S. "A Bond or Burden?: A Study of Shashi Deshpande's The Binding Vine", *Indian Women Novelists*: Set III: Vol.6. Dhawan R.K.(Ed) New Delhi: Prestige Books, 1995.

Jain, Jasbir and Amin, Amina. "Marriage As Purdah: Fictional Rendering of a Social Reality", *Margins of Erasure: Purdah in the Sub-Continental Novel in English.*

Jandial, Gur Pyari. "Evolving a Feminist Tradition: The Novels of Shashi Deshpande and Manju Kapur". *The Atlantic Literary Review,* Vol.4, No.3, July-September 2003.

Jha, Subhash K. "Coming to Terms with Tragedy", Rev. of The Binding Vine, *The Economic Times,* No. 30, 1994.

King, Adele. "Effective Portrait", *Debonair,* June 1988.

Mala, R. "Sexual Predicament and Shashi Deshpande's Women", *Indian Women Novelists*: Set I: Vol.V. Dhawan R.K. (Ed) New Delhi: Prestige Books, 1991.

Masal, N.B. "Shashi Deshpande's A Matter of Time: As An Exploration Of A Woman's Inner Life". Ed. by. T.M.J. Indra Mohan, *Shashi Deshpande: A Critical Spectrum*, New Delhi, Atlantic Publishers 7 Distributors, 2004.

Mathur, Malati. "Rebels In the Household", *India Today*, April 3, 2000.

Naikar, Basavaraj. "Joys And Sorrows of Womanhood In The Binding Vine, ed. by. Suman Bala, Khosla Publishing House: New Delhi, 2001.

Palkar, Sarla." Breaking The Silence: That Long Silence", *Indian Women Novelists* Set I. Vol: V, Dhawan, R.K.(Ed.) New Delhi: Prestige Books,1991.

Palkar, Sarla. Breaking the Shashi Deshpande's That Long Silence", *Feminism and Recent Fiction in English,* Singh, Sushila (Ed.). New Delhi: Prestige Books, 1991.

Patil, Ujwala. "The Theme of Marriage and Selfhood In Roots And Shadows", *Indian Women Novelists,* Set. I, Vol. V, ed. R.K. Dhawan, New Delhi: Prestige Books, 1991.

Paul, Premila. "The Dark Holds No Terrors; A Woman's Search for Refuge", *Indian Women Novelists,* ed. R.K. Dhawan, New Delhi: Prestige, 1991, Set. I, Vol.V.

Prasanna, A. Hari. "Image of Woman' in Shashi Deshpande's Fiction: A Study of Roots and Shadows and The Dark Hold No Terrors". *The Literary Voice.* No.3, February 1996.

Ramachandra, Ragini, Rev. of "The Dark Holds No Terrors", *The Literary Criterion,* Vol. XXI, Nos. 1 & 2, 1986.

Rani, T. Asoka. "Feminism Vis-à-Vis Woman's Dignity: A Study of Shashi Deshpande's That Long Silence". *The Journal of Indian Writing in English.*_Vol. 24, No.1 Jan 1996.

Roy, Evangeline Shanti. Shashi Deshpande's The Binding Vine: A Quest for the Anchor of Life". *Littcrit,* Vol. 27, No.1-2, June-December 2001.

Sahgal, Nayantara. "Women: Persons or Possessions", *Hindustan Times,* 19 July, 1970: iv.

Sahi, Rashmi. "Human Relationship in the Novels of Shashi Deshpande", *Indian Scholar,* Vol.15, No.2, July 1993.

Sahi, Rashmi. "Mother-Daughter Relationship in The Novels of Shashi Deshpande". *Indian English Literature:* Vol. II, ed. by Basavaraj Naikar, New Delhi: Atlantic Publishers and Distributors, 2002.

Sandhu, Sarabjit. "The Image of Woman in That Long Silence", *Indian Women Novelists,* Set. I Vol. V, ed. by. R.K. Dhawan, New Delhi: Prestige Books, 1991.

Sandhu, Sarbjit. "The Image of Woman in The Dark Hold No Terrors", *Indian Women Novelists* Set. I. Vol.V, Dhawan, R.K. (Ed.) New Delhi: Prestige Books, 1991.

Sathupati, Prasanna Sree. "Conflict and Identity in Shashi Deshpande's Novels", *Indian Women Novelists*: Set III: Vol.4 Dhawan R.K. New Delhi: Prestige Books, 1995.

Sethuraman, N. "Silence, Surrender and Compromise? A Study of Shashi Deshpande's That Long Silence", Sheshadri, Vena. "That Long Silence", Literature Alive, II, I, 1988.

Singh, Ranjini Jyothi. "Quest for Space and Selfhood in Shashi Deshpande's Small Remedies". *Pegasus,* Vol.4, Jan-Dec 2005.

Sivaraman, Gowri. "Self-Pitying Specimens Emerging as Self-Confident Neophytes In Some Writings Of Shashi Deshpande".

Swain, S.P. "The Unruffled Stream: Jaya in That Long Silence", *Creative Forum,* Vol.10, No.1-2, Jan-Dec 1997.

Tiwari, Shubha. "Women's Liberation Movement and Indian Women Novelists", *The Commonwealth Review.*Vol.19, No.2, 1997-1998.

# Index

**M**



**N**



**O**



**P**



**R**



**S**



**T**



**U**



**W**